PERSONAL ACCOUNTS I
NORTHERN IRELAND'S

PERSONAL ACCOUNTS FROM NORTHERN IRELAND'S TROUBLES

Public Conflict, Private Loss

Edited by Marie Smyth
and Marie-Therese Fay

Pluto Press

LONDON • STERLING, VIRGINIA

First published 2000 by Pluto Press
345 Archway Road, London N6 5AA
and 22883 Quicksilver Drive, Sterling, VA 20166–2012, USA

British Library Cataloguing in Publication Data
A catalogue record for this book is available from the British Library

ISBN 0 7453 1619 0 hbk

Library of Congress Cataloging in Publication Data
Personal accounts from Northern Ireland's troubles : public conflict,
private loss / edited by Marie Smyth and Marie-Therese Fay.
   p. cm.
  ISBN 0–7453–1619–0 (hc)
    1. Northern Ireland—History. 2. Victims of terrorism—
Northern Ireland—History—20th century. 3. Political violence—
Northern Ireland—History—20th century. 4. Social
conflict—Northern Ireland—History—20th century. 5. Violent
deaths—Northern Ireland—History—20th century. 6. Victims of
terrorism—Northern Ireland—Family relationships. 7. Northern
Ireland—Social conditions—1969– I. Smyth, Marie, 1953– II. Fay,
Marie-Therese, 1973–

DA990.U46 P515 2000
941.6—dc21

                                                          99–056756

05   04   03   02   01   00   5   4   3   2   1

Designed and produced for Pluto Press by
Chase Production Services, Chadlington, OX7 3LN
Typeset from disk by Stanford DTP Services, Northampton
Printed in the EU by TJ International, Padstow

Contents

Illustrations

Acknowledgements

We would like to thank the 85 adult interviewees and the young people who participated in the interviews. They welcomed us into their homes, and trusted us with their deepest experiences. We hope that we have not betrayed that trust. The support groups in this field helped us with our work, and we thank them; Survivors of Trauma, Ardoyne; Greencastle Women's Group; Damien Gorman, An Crann/The Tree; WAVE, Justice for the Forgotten, Dublin; young people from various communities in North and West Belfast, Derry and elsewhere. Our colleagues, Sarah Oakes, Mark Mulligan, Joy Dyer, Lisa Mitchell, Gwen Ford, Ann Boal, Grainne Kelly at the Cost of the Troubles Study, and fellow directors of the Cost of the Troubles Study, particularly David Clements, Brendan Bradley, John Millar, Hazel McCready, Sam Malcolmson, Sandra Peake, Marie McNeice, Mike Morrissey and Shelley Prue have provided assistance, guidance and feedback. Dr John Yarnell, Department of Public Health, Queen's University and the Health Promotion Agency; Dr Debbie Donnelly, NISRA; John Park, Social Services Inspectorate; Tony McQuillan, Northern Ireland Housing Executive; Dr Andrew Finlay, Trinity College Dublin; The Centre for Childcare Research at the Queen's University of Belfast; Arlene Healey from the Family Trauma Centre acted in advisory capacities to the project. We would like to thank Yvonne Murray, Linenhall Library, the staff in the Central Library, Belfast and Queen's University Library Belfast and our colleagues in INCORE, University of Ulster and United Nations University. We thank those who funded the research on which this book is based: the Central Community Relations Unit of the Central Secretariat; Making Belfast Work, North and West teams; the Special Support Programme for Peace and Reconciliation through the Northern Ireland Voluntary Trust; the Joseph Rowntree Charitable Trust; a private donation; Barnardo's Northern Ireland, Save the Children Fund; the Cultural Diversity Group of the Community Relations Council, the Belfast European Partnership Board, United States Institute for Peace and the Community Relations Council. We would also like to thank Belfast Exposed and Mervyn Smyth. We thank Alan Breen for his patience with the intrusion on his domestic life. Finally we thank Roger Van Zwanenberg and those at Pluto Press who published the book.

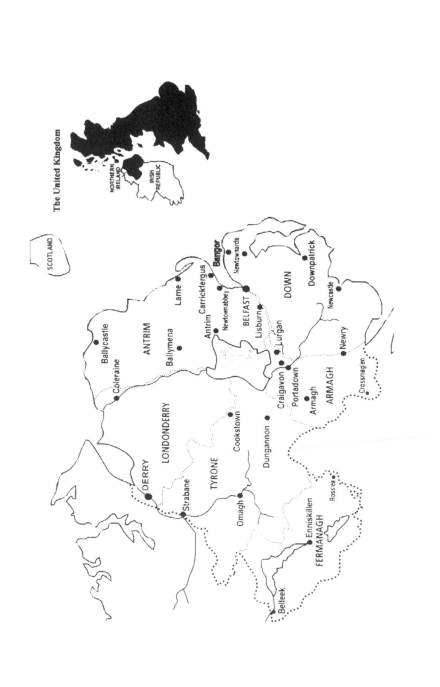

The United Kingdom

SCOTLAND

NORTHERN IRELAND

IRISH REPUBLIC

Ballycastle

Coleraine

Larne

ANTRIM

Ballymena

Carrickfergus

Antrim

Newtownabbey

Bangor

Newtownards

BELFAST

DERRY

LONDONDERRY

Lisburn

Lurgan

DOWN

Downpatrick

Strabane

Cookstown

TYRONE

Craigavon

Portadown

Newcastle

Omagh

Dungannon

Armagh

ARMAGH

Newry

Crossmaglen

Enniskillen

FERMANAGH

Rosslea

Belleek

Glossary

Abercorn Road   a road bounding the Protestant Fountain estate in Derry Londonderry city

Brits   British Army

Ballymurphy   an estate in Catholic West Belfast

Castlereagh   police interrogation and holding centre outside Belfast

The City   Hospital in Belfast

Cordite   an explosive gas associated with gunfire

Corrymeela Community   a Christian community which works for reconciliation in Northern Ireland

Crumlin, the Crum   prison in Belfast, used for shorter sentenced prisoners and those on remand

Dirty Protest   Republican prisoners, when campaigning for political status refused to wash, leave their cells or use the toilet facilities and in the end they smeared the walls of their cells with excreta

Duncairn Gardens   an interface between the Catholic and Protestant communities in North Belfast

Enclave   district solely inhabited by people of one political, social or religious group who are surrounded by a larger district inhabited by people of the other group

Glencairn   Loyalist estate in West Belfast

GP   General Practitioner, local doctor

Green Cross   organisation established to support Republican prisoners and their families

H-Blocks   The Maze Prison cell blocks – so-called because of their shape

Highfield   Loyalist estate in West Belfast

Hoods   local term used to refer to individuals involved in anti-social behaviour

INLA   Irish National Liberation Army

Internment   indeterminate detention in prison without trial, which operated from 1972 until 1975

IRA   Irish Republican Army

Kneecapped   shot in the knees

Long Tower   a Catholic area in Derry Londonderry city

The Maze   prison outside Belfast, also referred to as Long Kesh, the name it had when it was used as an internment camp

Musgrave   hospital in Belfast which specialises in orthopaedics, which also has a military wing

Newtownards Road	main road in the predominantly Protestant East Belfast
NIO	Northern Ireland Office
Peelers	the police, the RUC
Provos, Provies	Provisional IRA
Randalstown	A town about thirty miles from Belfast
Relatives Action Committee	group that campaigned for political status for Republican prisoners
Quare	big, remarkable
The Royal	hospital in Belfast
Toomebridge	a Catholic town about thirty miles from Belfast
Turf Lodge	Republican/Catholic area in West Belfast
RUC	Royal Ulster Constabulary
Saint Pat's, Saint Patrick's	Catholic borstal
Saracen	armed military vehicle used by British Army
Screws	Prison Officers
Shaftesbury Square	drug and alcohol clinic in Belfast
Shankill Butchers	Eleven Protestants known as the Shankill Butchers were sentenced to life imprisonment for nineteen murders and numerous other offences, after a series of random sectarian attacks on Catholics in the 1970s
Spamount Street	street in the Catholic New Lodge area
Stickies	Official IRA
The Fountain	Protestant enclave in the predominantly Catholic Derry City Centre
UDA	Ulster Defence Association
UDR	Ulster Defence Regiment, a regiment of the British Army, later disbanded and replaced by the Royal Irish Rangers
UFF	Ulster Freedom Fighters
Unity Flats	Catholic area at the bottom of the Protestant Shankill Road
UVF	Ulster Volunteer Force
'your man'	he, him, common way to refer to someone you are talking about, sometimes sardonically
Valium	anti depressant drug
Waterside	an area of the predominantly Catholic Derry Londonderry which is separated from the Catholic area by the river and which was predominantly Protestant until the mid-1990s. It is now roughly half Protestant, half Catholic
Whiteabbey	mixed village on outskirts of Belfast

Introduction

In the wake of cease-fires from 1994 onwards, a group of people from either side of the sectarian divide in Northern Ireland were brought together to discuss their position and possible contribution to the new political situation. What each member of the group had in common was their direct experience of being bereaved or injured in the Troubles. The growing determination amongst various groups in the population to have violence permanently ended was based on recognition of the damage done by the Troubles. Yet there was no reliable collated evidence of this damage, nor was there documentation of the needs that might have to be met should peace break out. This group formed 'The Cost of the Troubles Study', which became a limited company and a recognised charity. In partnership with researchers from the university sector, a study of the effects of the Troubles on the population was planned and initiated. The authors worked, as initiator and researchers on that project, and this book arises out of part of that work.

We saw our work as a kind of survey of the impact of the Troubles on the population. Our work involved both in-depth interviews and large survey work. When we began interviewing people about the effects of the Troubles on them, we thought about our interview technique, about the questions we should ask, and about the ways in which we would explain and analyse the 'data' we collected.

In a new climate of political change after the cease-fires, we began to interview people from a wide range of backgrounds and with a large spectrum of experiences. Through the process of interviewing people, we were unable to maintain that detached, professional stand. We were often moved to tears by what we heard. Frequently, we left with the memory of a story that would stay with us for months, maybe years afterwards. We would lie awake late at night, thinking about people we interviewed. We would wake in the early hours, thinking about story after story.

That engagement with the person we interviewed created for us a climate of intimacy in which the distance between the interviewer and the interviewed was temporarily reduced. We perceived ourselves as instruments, through which the interviewee's account could be documented. Both female, both from Catholic backgrounds, both civilians, we crossed a number of societal divisions in our work with the population of interviewees.

We were concerned that our representation of the human costs of the Troubles was representative of the total picture, so we used our earlier work as a guide. Both in absolute and relative terms, Catholics have been killed more often than Protestants, and the death rates per thousand are 2.5 per thousand for Catholics compared to 1.9 per thousand for Protestants using the 1991 Census of Population as a base. The same rates become 3.1 deaths per thousand for Catholics and 1.6 deaths per thousand for Protestants if an average of the 1971, 1981 and 1991 Census is used. Given that the Protestant population is larger than the Catholic population, we concluded that our selection of interviewees for this book reflected the impact of the Trouble on the two communities. Six of our interviewees are Protestant, seven are Catholic and one is from an ethnic minority. We do not present any interviews with those who had relatives killed in British security forces, nor with those who served in such forces, in spite of our attempts to conduct such interviews. Overall, we conducted 77 interviews, 44 with Catholics and 32 with Protestants, reflecting the death rates for the two religions. In gender terms, although 91.1 per cent of deaths in the Troubles were of males, this does not reflect the impact of injury and bereavement on women, so we conducted 43 interviews with males, and 34 with females. The geographical distribution was another consideration, given the con- centration of the impact of the Troubles on certain locations. Of the total interviewed, 24 lived in Belfast, ten in Derry Londonderry, 24 in small towns, three in border regions, five in rural areas, six in London and five in Dublin. This reflects the concentration of Troubles-related deaths and injuries, in Belfast, though perhaps under-represents the border regions, which were comparatively badly affected by the Troubles. In terms of age, one was under 16, two were between 16 and 21, 22 were between 21 and 40, 44 were between 41 and 60 and eight were between 61 and 80 years old.

By using information about the overall distribution of the impact of the Troubles in this way, we monitored our selection of interviewees, in order to ensure a reasonably representative selection of material. Whilst there will never be a completely satisfactory representation, we hope that the selection of accounts presented here provide both an 'inclusive enough' and a diverse overview of the human costs of the Troubles.

Interviewees were aware that they were not simply talking to us, but potentially to a wider public who would read what we wrote. Interviewees were also encouraged to talk freely and edit the transcript later if they wished to censor or add to what they told us in interview.

The heartbreaking and almost unbearable reality of extremes of loss is that, for the most part, the loss is irretrievable. No one can repair the damage, nothing can compensate.

People wanted to talk, to tell us about their experiences and the effects their experiences had on them. They barely needed our questions, they only required our attention. Most didn't want our help, although some accepted small services that were offered. Simply to listen was enough. It was important that we were strangers, that we had no reason to listen, beyond that we were interested in what people had experienced. It was also important that we worked with an organisation whose board was composed of people who knew what it felt like to suffer because of the Troubles. It was important that we were not journalists, and that we gave people signed undertakings that we would send them transcripts to edit and agree, and that they could change their minds about participation up until we published their interview in whole or in part. It was important that we emphasised that they could withdraw from participation, even after the interview had been conducted and transcribed. Several people made that choice, and we did not try to dissuade them from it.

In hindsight, for some, we may have performed the service of giving the story of their suffering a concrete and external form, as opposed to the internal form it had prior to the interview. Their story, in the form of a transcript, became separate from them, they could work with it, edit it. It had a beginning, middle, and, perhaps most importantly, it had an end. For some interviewees, for the first time, they weren't alone with their story – we were working on it with them. This was particularly true of the 14 interviews in this book and those included in the exhibition, 'Do You Know What's Happened?' which was launched in Belfast in November 1998. The preparation of these interview transcripts for publication required a close attention on our part to the text, and to the integrity of the story, so that the sense and emotional tone of what was conveyed to us in the interview was presented in the shorter version. We were treading on delicate ground and sensitivity to the feelings and views of the interviewee in the process of this editing was an exacting discipline.

During the project, a great deal of media interest was focused on the attitude of 'victims' to the early release of prisoners as part of the Good Friday Agreement. Several people we interviewed decided to be interviewed by the media for the first time after being interviewed by us. Some told us that their transcript was useful in helping them prepare for such interviews. Occasionally we were asked to be present during media interviews, and we either sat with them during such interviews or helped them to prepare for the interview. Having interviewed people, and talked to them through the course of sending and editing transcripts, we noted how we became protective of people we interviewed. Perhaps the intimacy of our interview contact with them had heightened our awareness of their potential vulnerability.

For some interviewees, this process of speaking out in public for the first time was empowering and built their level of confidence. It also had the effect of diversifying the range of voices in the public domain that were speaking publicly about the feelings of 'victims'. In the long term, we remain concerned that the development of public profiles can lead to victim-hood becoming incorporated into one's identity. However, it would be arrogant of us to presume to judge what is in the best interests of others. Those choices and decisions must be made by people themselves.

A colleague asked, on hearing of the interviews we were proposing to conduct, 'How will you know people are telling the truth?' The question implies that there is a singular truth, and only one way of perceiving issues or events. Particularly in relation to the most traumatic stories told to us, we noted that interviewees would tell the story again and again using identical language, almost as if the story was engraved on their mind. Tiny details, like the television programme that was on when a gun-man came in to kill a member of the household, or the item of clothing that someone was wearing at the time, seemed fixed in the mind of the witness of the most horrific events. On other occasions, one knew that the person was presenting a facet of events that avoided highlighting their own role or that of others. Whether such presentation is less true than another version is not a judgement we are equipped or prepared to make. We all tell ourselves stories about events that are compatible with our image of ourselves and tend to mask our own culpability and failings. It should not surprise us that interviewees do likewise. The events that are described in this book are told from the perspectives of the interviewees. Only some of the truths have been told. Some parts will be left out, since we interviewed only some of the participants and observers. This book contains some accounts, not every possible account. These accounts are as true as any others. They are sometimes contradictory, and we often got complicated answers to the two simple questions we asked: what has been your experience of the Troubles; and how have the Troubles affected you?

This book is produced for two main reasons. First, we are convinced that the general public are not aware of the true consequences of violence – the kind of violence that Northern Ireland has experienced over the last thirty years. The language that is used to present the impact of such violence to the general public – collateral damage, friendly fire and so on – conspires to sanitise and conceal the awful, gory and horrifying reality of the impact of war on the lives of ordinary people. Media coverage stops after a few days or weeks, allowing public consciousness to ignore the decades of consequences that follow a bombing or a shooting for those close to it.

This ignorance in the public consciousness is profoundly dangerous, since without a true awareness of its consequences, violence can seem an attractive way of dealing with conflict, competition or threat. Perhaps the only effective disincentive to the use of violence is an appreciation of its costs. That cost is not only paid by the individual victim, but also by families, communities and ultimately the society. Often the perpetrator, too, becomes a victim in the end.

The personal accounts in this book testify to all of this. At a time when violence is increasingly presented as entertainment, where gun-cultures proliferate and where armed conflicts can escalate seemingly overnight, a mature understanding of the consequences of violence has perhaps never been more important.

Secondly, Northern Ireland is a deeply divided society, containing limited opportunities for access to the experiences and views of those from the 'other side'. This book, and our exhibition, affords the reader access to the accounts of people they might never have the opportunity to meet; and even if they did meet, the possibility of being told and listening to their story would be limited by the deep divisions we live with. In the pages of this book, we have tried to provide access to the places and people we have had the privilege to listen to, recognising that fewer and fewer people in Northern Ireland have such privileged access as the divisions in the society deepen.

Finally, many of those we interviewed for this book told us that we were the first to listen to their account until they were finished talking. Yet many of the people we know who have suffered bereavement or injury in the Troubles express a need for public acknowledgement of their loss. Many bereaved or injured people feel neglected or forgotten, and some feel that their suffering has been meaningless in the context of cease-fires – that peace has come too late for them. This lack of acknowledgement of the human suffering, this sense of being forgotten, of not being cared about in the wider society is not only tragic, it is an indictment of the society itself. Furthermore, it sets up and maintains grievances on the part of those who have suffered. No community that wishes to sustain long-term peace can afford to remain indifferent to the isolation and suffering of any of its citizens, nor can the society afford to appear indifferent to such suffering. For it is such suffering and isolation that the grievances nursed over decades fester into the sores that erupt into violent conflict in the future. Uncomfortable, painful, shaming and heart-breaking as it may be to collect and read these accounts, the experiences contained in them must be known, acknowledged and available to a wider public. Only then can the various truths about the past and the various burdens the past has produced be more evenly distributed amongst us.

1 'The Troubles *is* my life'

Alice Nocher was interviewed in Bawnmore Greencastle, a Catholic enclave area in North Belfast in April 1997. Her brother was killed in 1975 in a bomb explosion. A couple of years later she was shot herself and survived. In 1983 her husband was shot dead in a sectarian attack whilst at work.

What really brought the Troubles home to me was the day my brother was killed. He worked to one o'clock that day and he came home. His two friends called for him. He went out and he never came back. Two o'clock there was an explosion and he and his two mates was killed.

I was working, and a woman came in and says that I was wanted at home immediately. I remember looking at her saying, 'Why?' And she said, 'You're wanted to comfort your mother.' I said I wasn't moving until she told me what was going on. So she says to me, 'Did you hear the explosion?' And I says, 'What explosion?' And she says, 'No, nothing. Just get your coat!' But it still didn't dawn on me that there was an explosion and my brother was involved in it.

I looked down and I seen all this rubble and I kept shouting to people I knew, 'What's wrong?' But nobody would tell me.

So then I got into the house and there was all sorts of doctors and nurses who just grabbed me and brought me into the working kitchen and gave me tablets. It was an awful day.

The lady that brought me home said, 'It was one of your brothers.' That's how I knew it was a brother. I had seven brothers. And when I got home I was looking at all their faces to see which brothers I could see. 'Cause no one would tell me which one it was. I remember seeing my brother Pat and says, 'It's not Pat!' And then I seen Frank, 'It's not Frankie!' and all down the line like that. And then I heard my mummy squealing, 'My Sammy, my Sammy!' That's how I knew it was Sammy.

My mummy was actually crawling the walls in the living room. She was on the settee crawling the walls squealing for her son. They sedated my mummy. That was one of the worst times.

7

1. Alice Nocher in her home in September 1999. Photograph: Marie Smyth

I remember after he was buried, I remember going in night after night trailing her out of his room. It just went on and on.

I used to have to bring her walks at three in the morning just to get her out of the house.

Everybody was wrapped up in their own grief for him. My life totally changed. It was like the end of family life as we knew it.

As I say, these doctors and all were giving tablets. But I was the eldest girl, so they said to me, 'You have to be strong for your mother.' I wanted to go to pieces. But, you know, I had to be strong for her. They gave me a glass of water and two tablets. I was shaking that much, one of the nurses had to take it and hold it to my mouth to get the tablets down.

I felt I wasn't allowed to cry or do anything like that, in case I upset my mummy or anything. I cried, but very rarely. I held it all back really. I just kept going over in my mind as to who could have left that there. I was angry at the ones who left it there. I was angry, I was hurt. It was a mixture of everything.

I tried to get someone to blame but when you can't find someone to blame you start saying, 'Maybe if he had've stayed at work or if he had've stayed and had that cup of tea.' If, if, if. It's not going to change anything. They had whole lives ahead of them.

My mummy didn't get any help really either. Because after the initial shock and the doctors and all left that was it. You were left to cope. Other than the neighbours calling in, no one came near us.

But I didn't go to that inquest. I'm not even sure whether my mummy went, but my daddy definitely went. Because my poor daddy had to identify him. It took my daddy an awful long time to get himself together again. My brother wasn't really mutilated too badly. He'd lost his legs and his arm and half of his head. But the other lad was absolutely in bits and pieces. And I thought it was very cruel. Because when they went to identify the bodies, the policeman or whatever threw a black bag up on the table and says, 'Identify your son!' My daddy was able to identify my brother because compared to the other two he wasn't that badly mutilated. I thought that was the cruellest of things to do. And my daddy couldn't get over it. He used to disappear every night and when he came back from his pigeon shed you could see he'd been crying. But that was the man's thing to do. You don't cry in front of women. But you could see every night, nobody ever said to him, 'Were you crying?' He just come back and we knew. And that went on for a long long time. Long time. It was an awful strain. Awful strain.

I remember going to work. After that they gave me an awful time where I worked. They stopped me and said, 'We're going to do you!' And they sort of branded the family 'Provo bastards' or you know 'scum of the earth' and all this. Well I was really really frightened. I knew something bad was going to happen if I didn't get out of it. They were going to do this and that to me. In between times I went and looked for another job myself. And I came home from work on the Friday and there was a letter to say to start at Abbey Meat Packers on the Monday. So I said that I was going to work there. And that was another wrong move.

I remember going in and crying my eyes out the whole day 'cause my brother had worked there and I'd another brother worked there at the time. I remember going up to him and crying my eyes out the whole lunch time. And after a week or two I got back into a routine and everything was OK. And then we were shot down there going to work one morning.

This is me and my best friend Margaret. And there was three young lads in the car. We got into the car and Margaret and I were fighting about who was going to get into the back seat. There was only two doors on the car. I says, 'Auch, I'll get in first.' And I was the only one to survive it. So actually, by me getting into that seat first really saved my life.

We left in the car and we went along to Whiteabbey. And we turned up Glenville Road and he sort of jerked the car and stopped suddenly.

We were half asleep in the back seat you know, and I actually thought he had hit someone. And I says 'What's wrong?' And the next thing the door was opened and he shouted, 'Get out, get out to fuck!' And I looked out and there was a car pulled up in front of us and there were men getting out with guns. And just looking at it, I knew it was us they wanted.

I remember saying, 'We're not going to get out of this!' There were only two doors in the car and we were trapped. I looked at Margaret and I says, 'What are we going to do?' And Margaret says, 'Lie down, lie down!' I can't describe the terror that went through me. It was terrifying. The thoughts that came into my mind was that I'm too young to die. I was just frozen on the spot.

The boy at the end tried to get out. He pushed the seat forward to get out and they shot him. And the other two got away, thank God. So that just left Margaret and I in the car. So they riddled the car with a sub-machine-gun. It seemed like an eternity, I heard the shooting. But they were actually shooting at the lads running down the street. And then I felt pain, like a burning sensation. And I remember as each bullet hit me, it lifted me off the seat. So when we were in a lying down position, as the bullets hit, we were sitting up. At one stage my head hit the ceiling of the car. It lifted me that high.

I was hit in my arm, two in my hip, one in my thigh. One in my leg, foot and ankle. One in my hand. Eight times altogether.

And I remember when it was over, like a burning smell in the car, like someone had struck a match, but far stronger. But the police told me later, that was the smell of them going through the metal.

But I remember it just went silent. I rolled down onto the floor. And I remember Margaret saying, 'Get up, get off me, you're hurting me!' And with my good arm I lifted myself up. I remember shouting out 'Help us! Help us! Somebody help us!'

These people lifted us out of the car and left us on the pavement. I heard Margaret shouting my name a few times.

Margaret lived for a week. She died a week later in hospital. I knew in my own heart she was bad. And someone says she was only an arm's length away from me on the pavement, but I couldn't see her. And I kept calling for her and all.

I thought Margaret and I would be together in the ambulance. But it wasn't. It was the wee boy of sixteen. And that terrified me, because he was on one side of the ambulance and I was on the other. He was shot in the head. And I could see this. And he was breathing very deeply. He was really fighting for breath. And the ambulance man was attending to him. And then he turned round and he started to dress my wounds. And I said, 'No! See to him, he needs you more than I do!' And he just looked at me and said, 'You are a very brave wee girl.' And I says, 'I'm not brave, he needs you more than I do.' And he says, 'There is no more I can do for him love.' And that was awful, I felt useless. I couldn't help him or anything.

And then I heard later three o'clock that day or something, he died. I remember the journey [in the ambulance] because it passed this way and I was looking out the window. So, if I could see my family just one person, a brother, anyone just to see them. And the strangest things go through your head. I thought maybe they were following us to the hospital to shoot us again. I didn't feel it was over in that way. And even in the hospital after they'd operated and all I never felt secure the whole time I was there. I kept thinking they would come in and do it again.

When we got to hospital I heard Margaret again in the next bed shouting my name. And they asked me was I in much pain. And I said, 'Yes' and they gave me morphine or something. By this time my family were there. So the first one I seen was my daddy. My daddy came over and kissed me and told me I was going to be all right and that. And then I saw Margaret's daddy. And I just told him the truth. And he says, 'Don't you worry about that. You just worry about getting yourself better!'

So then I was brought into the operating theatre. And then when I was put into a ward my daddy came in to see me. And I said to him I was shot at least seven times. And my daddy went out and told my mummy and she practically called him a liar. She says, 'Don't be stupid, you'd be dead if you were shot that many times!' And then they went and asked the doctor, and the doctor said that was right. And they just couldn't believe it that someone could be shot that many times and survive it.

The doctor used to come round, and he said Margaret was coming on great. And then on the following Monday about three o'clock he says, 'You had a wee friend in intensive care?' And I says, 'Yes!' And I was waiting for good news. And he says, 'She died at two o'clock today.'

I was just devastated. I knew she was bad but I always thought she would pull through. He says, 'She'd died.' I never seen her after that. I wanted them to bring me down to see her but they wouldn't let me. The first time they got me up I fainted with the pain. And I couldn't go to the toilet myself, so I used bed pans and stuff. And being young I detested it.

Sleep was really – it was very hard to sleep. And when I did sleep it was all bad nightmares and very, very bad dreams. Woke up in sweats. It did go on for a while.

I remember coming home that day and I couldn't believe this. Right in front of us on the motorway was a hearse with a coffin in it. And the tears just flowed right down my face. Because Margaret had been buried that day and they wouldn't let me out for the funeral. And there it was just travelling in front of us. It broke my heart. Because I was saying to myself, 'That could have been me going home.' I remember looking and I could see my daddy's eyes through the mirror and he was crying, knowing I was crying and that was the way it went on.

For when I got out of hospital I had to go down to the doctors. Mummy made me, because I wasn't sleeping or anything and I'd lost weight. I was always a very thin girl, you know, in my teens. But my weight went right down to seven stone four or something. My hair was falling out. And when I went down to the doctor he told me 'to run away on – I was lucky that my hair didn't turn white over night'. And that was the sympathy I got from the doctor. He says, 'It will recover itself – it was the shock, you don't know how lucky you are!' Well I did know how lucky I was. I didn't need him or anyone else to tell me. But this is all you got. Getting up in the morning and there was bunches of hair and my hair was down to my waist when I was young. It was just lying on the pillow.

And I was afraid to wash it. That went on for about a year I think. I can't remember really. But it did grow back itself, eventually

[I got] no help from anyone and they just didn't want to know. Then it was about a month after that my daddy said, 'Come on. I'm bringing you to the doctor right now.' The least wee noise I was hiding behind the settee and I was going up to my room at night and putting the wardrobe over the door. So I went to a different doctor and he said I was going through a breakdown and as I was actually talking to the doctor I wasn't looking at him. I was looking at the door to see who was coming in the door. And he noticed this and he says, 'There is no one coming in the door Alice. No one is going to hurt you again.' And he said to my daddy 'She's going through a breakdown and I want you to get her away not tomorrow, not next week, tonight.'

So my daddy put me on a plane to England that night. And I stayed with my brother. I went over there and as we were going along this road I was still jumping at every car going by and they were laughing at me saying 'It's not like that over here.' And then it suddenly dawned on me that it's not! This is a different place. And I relaxed. And I came home a lot better. I stayed about a month.

But I fell and I broke my plaster in half. So I went to their hospital over there. And I'll never forget their attitude towards me. 'What happened to you?' 'I was shot.' And automatically they assumed I was guilty of something. And I was treated like absolute dirt. So within three days I had myself home.

I was terrified to come back. I didn't want to go through that again, sitting in my room and not going out. I wanted to be on my own. I kept thinking to myself – if they do come in to shoot anyone I would be more of a hindrance than help. Because they would be that busy looking after me they would get themselves killed. I couldn't understand. 'Why?' I asked myself that question. The UFF, they said they done it. It was a bus load of soldiers and their wives in England and there was a couple of them killed. They said they shot us in retaliation for that bus. And I was saying to them, 'What bus?' Didn't even know about this bus.

There was a court case some years later and I was subpoenaed to go as a witness and there were three fellas standing in the dock. Their faces were covered anyway. They were masked. And that was terrifying because I had to relive that all over again. And in the end they got off. I said to the detective 'Why did you put me through that knowing that you hadn't enough evidence to convict these people?' He says he thought there might have been a chance.

The judge was very sympathetic. It was absolutely terrifying. I had to get up to walk round them to the stand. I would like to have been able to say they are the guilty ones. It was the detective who said to me they were the ones that done it, though he couldn't prove it.

I don't know where I got the courage from. I just stared straight back at them and I stared into every one of their eyes and they sort of looked at me and turned away. They looked everywhere but me. I felt I was the strongest of us all for doing that. After the hearing Margaret's daddy put his arms round me and he says, 'I'm so very proud of you for being able. Even when you were being sworn in when you had the Bible in your hand you didn't even shake.' I says, 'I was literally shaking inside.' He says, 'It didn't show.' So that was a wee boost, him saying he was proud of me. But it is wonderful where you get the strength from. Because I kept saying, 'Mummy, I can't get up there, I can't get up there.' She says, 'You'll get up and you'll do what you have to.' And I did.

I had no teenage life. I just locked myself in my room every night. Didn't know what it was like to go out. I was afraid. I remember going into the post office to get my sickness benefit and couldn't stand in the queue for shaking that much. I had to leave. I took, like, agoraphobia or something. Everything that was so simple before was an ordeal. Just stayed in the house. All my teenage years just wasted away. Just every day got that wee bit easier, but it took time. It wasn't like going home one day and getting on with it.

After about a year I started pulling myself together because I did go through that sort of a breakdown and that was an awful hard time. But once I got over that, then I started getting on with my life. A friend of mine came by one night and he brought me down to the place I was shot and that terror of coming up that street. I remember squealing at him, 'Don't you dare bring me to this place!' But he just brought me right by and he says, 'Look, it's OK.' And then I was able to go back after that. I just thought that that car was going to be there and that same thing was going to happen. It is hard to describe. I know you go through it within a second or so but it was that fear of it happening again. I often said, 'Look, you could maybe go through it once and survive it, but you could never go through it twice and survive it. Never.' I don't believe you could. That went on even after I got married and had my children.

And then when my husband was killed it sort of came back with a vengeance if you like. I had three children and was pregnant with my fourth. He worked part time in a butcher's shop. And it was a Saturday morning he went into the bathroom and got washed and he shouts, 'I'll see you later Alice!' I said, 'All right!' And away he went. And about quarter to ten, ten o'clock, my sister knocked at the door. She says, 'Alice, are the kids dressed?' I said, 'No, they are still in bed with me.' She says, 'Give me their clothes.' I said, 'Why?' Then I seen the priest coming behind her and I went, 'Oh, not again! Not again!' And I ran away up the stairs. I didn't want to know. I thought I'd went through enough. I couldn't go through this again. She shouted up, 'It's Davy. He's been shot.' I thought maybe it's only on the knees or leg or something. She didn't answer. And I ran down the stairs and the priest was standing in the living room and I says, 'What hospital is he at?' And they still didn't answer. And I knew then. And the priest said 'Alice, I'm sorry to tell you this. Davy is dead.' And I remember squealing or something.

Apparently he was cleaning the windows in the shop and this car went by that was watching the shop for some time. Well, apparently they were to go in the shop and just shoot whoever was in the shop. But Davy had been out to clean the windows. So that is what took them so long. But as Davy finished cleaning the windows and went back in, one of the young girls that worked in it said, 'There is a bit in the corner you missed.' So he went back out to clean this wee bit in the corner. And meanwhile the car had stopped round the side and they came running round the corner not expecting to see Davy at the window again. They thought he was in the shop. But as Davy seen them and the guns, he jumped down off the stool and went to run. And as he ran, they shot him in the back. And he died there as he fell. But in a way he saved the rest of their lives. Because their plan, apparently, was to walk in to the shop and shoot everyone that was in it. There was only a wee young girl about sixteen there. So in a way he saved their lives.

They didn't tell me much. Looking back on it. Apparently when they told me he was dead, I just assumed he was in some sort of morgue or hospital. But I didn't know that all this time he was lying down the front of the road with a blanket over him. Every time I asked them where he was, nobody would tell me. But if I had've knew he was there I would have been down there. But maybe that is the reason they didn't tell me.

But the priest and my sister-in-law were just the two in the house then. Then other people started coming in. My mummy came in and my sister.

Daniel was three, David was five turning six. And what do you say to wee ones? I wasn't prepared. I remember sitting on the settee and they crawled up on my knee crying. And I remember saying to them, 'It'll be all right, it'll be all right, daddy has just gone to heaven. We'll be all right.'

I felt devastated that it could happen to me again. Didn't think it was fair. And I kept saying, 'Why me?' I think that was the first time I really ever questioned God. 'Why me? What have I done?' God forgive me looking back on it, but they say it's all part of the healing. I don't know. And I just didn't think it was fair that I should go through this again. I remember, after having my baby there was visiting time in the hospital and all their husbands came in. I was devastated. I got up and I pulled the curtains round my bed and got into bed and just cried like a baby. And then my mummy came up and my husband's mummy came up, but it wasn't the same. I just wanted everybody to go away and let me have this good old cry.

I remember crying and one time a nurse came in and just in passing she would sympathise and say, 'I know what you mean.' She was getting married and her boyfriend was killed, and there was someone who knew what I was going through really. We had something in common. And she would have kept me company and talked me round a bit. It wasn't much but it was a help. Because you can't really go up to a complete stranger and say, you know.

I was never as glad to get home from anywhere. It was hard. I had plenty of help for the first six weeks but after that, I found decisions hard, even in just giving him a name. Because I couldn't talk that over with my husband, which I thought was very important, giving him a name. And other wee decisions about school, I found that an awful burden taking these decisions myself. I got used to it.

I moved back home after a while to my old house. I tried to change it as much as possible, got different carpet and different wallpaper so it wouldn't be exactly the same. But it was still those four walls. It was very, very hard financially as well as emotionally 'Am I going to have enough for tomorrow night's dinner? Someone needs shoes.' And that is the way it went on. His father buried him. He told me to put in a claim for compensation, because he was working part time. But how they got out of that one was I wasn't entitled to legal aid. I hadn't the money to bring them to court. So that was it.

The police told me it was definitely the Loyalists that done it but no one ever claimed it. Not even to this day. No one has ever claimed killing him. There were stages there I hated them and times I even felt sorry for them. Did they not know what they are doing? Like they have to go to meet the Lord their maker with that on their conscience. I've had so many different feelings over the years. Now I just don't feel nothing for them.

I had very, very good friends, Protestant friends. I went to their homes and I worked with them and I felt bitter for a while after he was shot. I didn't trust them. Because I was told it was someone in work that had set us up. But I didn't blame anyone in particular. You know, I just take people as I find them and you know if they are OK by me, I'm OK by them. Live and let live.

But it would be a different thing, I suppose, if you put one of them in front of me and said, 'He definitely did this or did that.' The police have yet to come to my house to tell me my husband is dead. Or they've yet to come to my mummy and daddy and tell them I was shot. That was left for neighbours. The only time they came round after I got shot was to come to get a statement after I got out of hospital. As I say, the priest told me when my husband was killed. No police ever came near the door. Never.

I was only getting £40 a week or something. Couldn't afford much. Got Paul to school. It was £16 a week they wanted for dinner money because I wasn't entitled to free meals. And it just got to the stage I couldn't send them to school. I just hadn't got the money. It was either eat a lunch at the school or eat nothing when they came home. And I deliberately kept them off. The school educational officer came out and said, 'Why have you not been sending your children to school?' And I says, 'I can't afford to'. He says, 'Is that the only reason they are off?' I said, 'Yes.' I says, 'You want £16 of that for school meals.' Says I, 'I haven't got it.' He says, 'You just send your children to school, and I'll make sure they get a lunch.'

It is a cruel world. But I think if you had financial help, it would make it that much easier. Because for to get one of them a pair of shoes, you've to save up for weeks. And in that time maybe somebody else needed a pair. And this is the way it was going on. A constant battle.

My main concern for the children was when they grew up. I was afraid of them being bitter and joining some organisation and finding themselves in prison for a long time. Or worse, dead. So I always tried to be honest, but play it down if you like, so that they wouldn't be bitter. Like I would say to them 'There are good Protestant people, just the way there are good Catholic people. And there are bad Catholic people and there are bad Protestants.'

And then they know I'd got shot myself, and that would make it worse.

I remember my wee boy not long after his daddy died. I had to bring him to a child psychologist because he had a lot of problems. And he said to me one night, 'When I grow up, I'm never going to work.' I says, 'You're not going to work? Why?' He says, 'Well my daddy was shot working and you were shot going to work so I'm not going to work.' That threw me. I didn't know what to say. I tried to explain it was just unfortunate, wrong place, wrong time, things like that. I didn't know what to say to the child. It was a hard thing to answer. Because it was the truth.

I wanted to take the kids away after he died. And when I said I wanted to go, they said to me, 'Don't.' I only had that one experience about the hospital in England but they said, 'Stay home, rear your family. To go over there to strangers, away from your family to people who don't know you. They don't want to know you.' They sort of talked me out of that, to stay here. And I'm glad I did. It would be a great wee county if there was no trouble.

Even now, I've a big lad, there, of eighteen. David is such a good lad, but I want to know where he is going, and what time he'll be in. Who is he with? Even when he was working in the training centre up the road, I was terrified of him going walking that road in the mornings. Because he's still my child, but to the outside world he's probably a man. If he were to go away to work in Belfast or somewhere I would be petrified. But then I say, well it [the Troubles] did happen. And this is where you are and this is where you are staying.

But it has taken over my whole life. It has been my whole life. I think time is a great healer. You don't forget anything. It just helps. I am a lot calmer today than I was then. I would say I was stronger for all that. I think I have to be strong. I wouldn't have survived it if I hadn't been. Because there has been manys a time I've sat with a bottle of pills in my hand. 'Take these pills.' But a strong person goes on. If I had of been a weak person I would have fell to the wayside. But I'm a lot calmer and stronger for all that experience. Although I could have been doing without it.

I'm always conscious of the fact that things could happen when I am out. Like I keep saying to my daughter, 'If you are going for a taxi, don't stand outside, they could go by and riddle the taxi.' And I'm sure I had the kids' heads away. 'Don't stand outside it. Sort of walk up and down. Don't stand in the one place.'

I think this is the longest I've ever talked about it to anybody. You're scared of people getting fed up listening to you. People had their own worries and probably their own tragedies, especially round this area. An awful lot has happened to people round here. Directly or indirectly they've been hit in some way or the other. And people were trying to cope with their own lives, they hadn't time to listen to you.

Or I find, if you were talking, they were actually thinking of their own troubles. They might have agreed with you now and again, but that was it.

To talk about it is to remember about it. People don't want to remember. But it happened, and it is never going to go away.

2   Multiple Bereavement and Loss

Margaret Valente was interviewed in the office of Cost of the Troubles Study in May 1997. Her brother-in-law was killed in a Republican feud in 1975, and his wife died four years later, unable to cope with her husband's death. Margaret then lost her own husband, when he was killed by the IRA as an alleged informer. She later was the first on the scene when her daughter's partner was shot dead in a sectarian attack.

Well I was about sixteen when I became aware that Northern Ireland was different. And it was mostly other fellas about that age, sixteen or seventeen – they started to talk about the fact that we had no councillors representing us on the council, and about all the discrimination that went on within Northern Ireland. Until that, I didn't really know what it was about. I wasn't interested in it even. So then I suppose about 1967 or 1968, you began to realise there was violence. There were riots in Divis Street then.

I was living in Ballymurphy then, but I would've stayed down the Lower Falls in Divis Street. I remember going to the riots there. In Ballymurphy you never really saw parades and bands, so there wasn't much sectarianism. I got married in 1969 and moved to Unity Flats. It was a real big difference, because the Shankill was out the side of Unity Flats, and every Saturday there were riots. And then the police would have always come in to Unity Flats and beat us, put on the water cannons and things like that. There was a man killed there too. He was beat to death by the police. McCrory – he was an old man. I'll always remember it, and he was just caught up in the riot and he was killed.

I had my first baby in 1969 and I had another one in 1970. And there was a real bad riot on the Shankill Road and a policeman was killed on the Shankill Road – Arbuckle you called him. At this stage, the soldiers weren't in North Belfast; they were on the Falls Road. We had no soldiers at all, and the crowds in the Shankill were really, really angry. It was really bad that night. It was the first time I was very frightened.

The barricades went up in 1970 at Unity Flats and that was to keep Loyalists out of the flats. It was frightening. I used to watch people in the middle of the night taking their children out. I always stayed in the flat but we used to look out and see people taking their children – six, seven or eight year olds – over to the chapel and staying out with them when the trouble was getting so bad.

So then, the soldiers were sent in then. The next morning you woke up and the soldiers were there and they had nowhere to sleep. They were all sleeping in the streets and people were out giving them cups of tea and sandwiches. We were so glad to see the soldiers coming in.

I never wanted to stay. I wanted to get out, live in England, or down South, anywhere at all. My husband wouldn't move, he wanted to stay where he was born. He was very Nationalist/Republican minded and they were always having big debates in our house about the police and the government. They were all very aware, politically.

I think you felt safe when the barricades went up. It was safe because nobody could get in then at night-time. Then when internment started, that's when they moved the barricades. And the police used to come in at nights with soldiers and just run into people's houses, raid the houses and take people out of their homes, you know. So then we started a vigilante group.

You couldn't let the men be vigilantes, because they just lifted the men, so there was no point. So the women used to do it, on a rota basis. Some women would go out at 12–2 a.m. in the morning. Some would have went back to bed then at 2 a.m. and someone would have come out from 2 a.m.–4 a.m. That was all the bin lid stuff. If the soldiers came into the area and we were about, we banged the bin lids and blew the whistles and got everybody up in the area.

My husband was never interned. He worked on the Newtownards Road and I used to really worry about him going to work, because it was the time of the Shankill Butchers. I used to put the two kids in the pram and walk down to the city centre and wait for him getting off the bus. I used to think he was going to be killed. It was tension all the time.

You got a lot of abuse from soldiers. Shouting things after you in the streets. Calling you all sorts of names or stopping and searching you. They didn't physically search you, but the policewomen would have searched you, making remarks while they were doing it and just making you feel generally like shit, that you weren't worth anything.

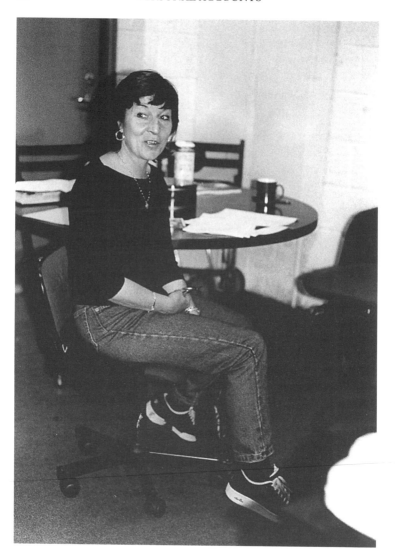

2. Margaret Valente pictured in the office of the Cost of the Troubles
Study, September 1999. Photograph: Marie Smyth

I knew a lot of people that were killed by the soldiers, by the
IRA in feuds, and by Loyalists. The Relatives Action Committee
was a group set up to help prisoners, to get political status for the
prisoners. So I joined that. I felt good about that, because you felt

as if you were doing something. You were protesting and standing in the streets giving out leaflets. That's how I knew a lot of people that had been killed, because they would have been in it. My husband was involved with Sinn Fein.

In 1975, my brother-in-law was killed in a feud between the 'stickies' [the Official IRA] and the 'Provos' [Provisional IRA]. That was really awful, when he was killed, because it was his own people, and people he knew really well that walked into the house and shot him. My sister was there when they came in and shot him. She opened the door, and they just came in and killed him, sitting in the living room. She was expecting her second baby and the other one was only about a year and a half.

I went up to see her at my mother's house and she was just sitting on the hearth, just staring, not saying anything, just constantly biting her fingernails. Every time she cried, it was, 'Don't be crying! Take this tablet.' She was sedated all the time. At the time you thought that was OK, but now thinking back on it, I think she should have been allowed to grieve and shout about it.

She lived in the area. She knew who killed her husband, but she couldn't say who killed him, because my brothers all lived there and my father lived in the area, so they would have had to leave the country. They wouldn't have been able to stay. So she couldn't really say anything about who killed them. She saw his killers every day and they used to scare her to make sure she kept her mouth closed.

Her husband was killed on the 3rd November, and her son was born on the 23rd December. When he was born, she just had no interest in him at all. She just didn't want anything to do with him really. Then she started the drink and she didn't eat.

The day that her wee baby was getting christened, she didn't go to the chapel, she said she didn't feel well. Everybody went to the christening and she took an overdose. It was just by chance another sister of mine, who didn't know we were away, went up to the house and found her. Then she was in Purdysburn for a while. They were talking to her about why she done all this stuff. Everybody knew why she done it, you know.

I think it was the guilt she felt, because she opened the door. I mean physical things started happening, like ulcers, and then she started taking fits. She was something like five stone. That's how skinny she got. There was nothing you could do. She became very bad tempered and angry and if you tried to help her it was, 'Shut up' or, 'Get out of the house.' One evening she lifted a bin and hit my dad on the head with it, and split his head open. She wouldn't have been like that before. She just lost interest in her children. But my mother was there and my sister, who was a year older than her, she took a lot to do with the children. She'd have bathed them and put them to bed and looked after them. So they had other people's help.

It just devastated our whole family and that really made me very angry. I looked at my sister, who was suffering really badly. We were on our way to our holiday and getting on the train, when my father came along and I knew by his face something was really bad and she was dead. She was found dead in the house. The police thought that she had overdosed but she hadn't. It was a massive convulsion. We just didn't really understand what she was going through. I knew she was hurting really badly. My father just was never the same again either. He seemed to lose vitality and something about him was never the same again.

I used to say to my husband, 'If you ever get involved with them [paramilitaries] or go to jail I'll never go to see you. I'm taking the children and I'm leaving here and never coming back again.' But then he did get involved with them anyway, although I didn't know he was involved. I knew he was in Sinn Fein, and that was OK because it was political. But I didn't want him to be involved in killing people or have any part in killing people. But apparently he did. I didn't know about it until after he was killed. I had no idea. I knew he was involved with them ones, like, putting posters up and going to the meetings and organising protests and political stuff. It was a shock that he was that deeply involved in it all.

It was on a Wednesday and we went round to the community centre. We used to go round to the community centre and say Masses for the hunger strikers. So I was round that evening, anyway, and we were going to a candlelight procession on the Falls Road that night. This was November, and Peter says to me, 'You mightn't be able to go to that procession tonight. I might have to go out.' And I said, 'Why do you have to go out?' And he said, 'Somebody might call for me.' And I said, 'Why?' And asked him all the questions. He said, 'Look I don't know, I mightn't go, but just in case.'

He was decorating the living room, we were decorating it for Christmas and we'd all the paper stripped off and everything. A fella came to the door and he said to me, 'I'm going to have to go.' He got his coat and I asked him when he'd be back. He said, 'I'll be in later on, don't wait up on me, but I will be in later on.'

I'd no phone and my youngest, she was only a year and a half at this stage, and my sister had taken her to Ballymurphy. Now I was waiting on Peter coming back and waiting on her coming back, and by 11 o'clock nobody had come back. I was getting very, very worried. So I knocked the neighbour's door and used the phone and somebody said my sister was on her way down with the baby. So she came in anyway and Peter still hadn't come in. So she said, 'Sure that procession's on up the Falls Road. He's maybe met up with people or is sat up there having a drink.' So I made his lunch up for work the next day and then went to bed. I woke up the next morning and he still wasn't in. I went to work anyway and I came back, and he still wasn't home.

I was vomiting, I was constantly sick. So I sent for his brother, and I said what are we going to do? I said I was going to phone round places, police stations, anywhere at all and see if I can find him. I couldn't get out of the house because I had four kids and couldn't just go off and leave them. So he went to the Tavern, a bar in the Flats to phone all the police stations. And I said to phone the Law Society and find out if the police have him. Maybe the police lifted him and he's in Castlereagh [Interrogation Centre] because he'd been lifted three or four times previously and took to Castlereagh. They used to come in and raid the house and take him away. So he rang everywhere and he came back and he says, 'No! He's not there!'

So this fella came into the house that my husband knew, and I knew as well and he said to me, 'I was up in the Falls Road there, Peter is in the Falls Road. I was talking to him and he's OK. He says he'll see you later tonight or tomorrow.' So I felt this was good. He's all right and he's going to come home.

So Friday came and he still hadn't come back. Again, his brother phoned all these places and looked up the Falls Road to see if anybody had seen him. So on the Friday night, I was to go down and collect the Green Cross for the prisoners' relatives. I was going out the door and it was really pouring with rain, really bad night, and this fella was at the door and he had one of them coats with a hood on, all zipped up. I didn't know this man. He said, 'Look, I was talking to Peter, I was at a training camp, and as I was coming out of the training camp he was going in.' And here's me, 'That's not right, he wouldn't.' Friday morning had came and I'd no money or wages, I'd no money in the house. I knew he wouldn't do this. He wouldn't just leave me with no money. He would get in touch with me; it was just totally out of character.

So on Friday night, I was sitting in the house and all the kids were in bed and the 9 o'clock news came on and it said there was a body found in Highfield, a man in his early thirties. And I just knew it was him, I just knew. And I said, 'What am I going to do?' And I couldn't think of anything to do.

So at this time in Unity Flats, like in most areas in Belfast, they had set up caravans where they had set up all night vigils in support of the hunger strikers. At this time the first hunger strike was still going on. So I went and sat in the caravans for something to do. And people were talking about this body that was found in Highfield. And they were saying they were talking to such and a person and they thought it was such and such, giving these names of who they thought it was. So I thought, 'I'm going to have to say it's Peter.'

So I went home anyway and I went to bed. And I was lying dozing and then sort of waking up and I didn't know what to do exactly. I didn't want to go out and say to people that it was Peter, in case I was wrong. I was in bed and I heard footsteps along the landing and I heard bang, bang, bang on the door. I ran up because I thought it was Peter, but there was nobody there, nobody at all. I thought that was really weird.

So the next morning was Saturday. And the door knocked and I went down. And it was his sister. She asked had Peter not come home and I said, 'No! What am I going to do? I've to buy food and I've no money!' I told her there was that body found last night. And she said, 'No, it wouldn't be', so not to worry about it. Then his friend from work came with Peter's wages, because he said Peter never came in for his wages. Then the police came to the door. They just said to me, 'Are you Margaret Valente?' And I said, 'Yes.' And I said, 'Is it about the body in Highfield? It's Peter isn't it?' And he just said, 'Yes, it is your husband.' And that was it.

His body came home on the Saturday and all my walls had been stripped of wallpaper. So all my neighbours came in and took the washing off the line and put it in covers. And they took my children out of the house and brought them round to their houses. They came in with paper and paint and painted the whole living room. They brought in dishes and cups and pots and pans, tea towels and all that stuff. They organised everything, they were great. But at the time I thought this was an awful invasion of my privacy. People just took over your house.

It was that night, at the wake, I could hear people in the kitchen talking, and I could hear my cousins saying, 'It was in the *Belfast Telegraph* tonight, and the police are saying it isn't sectarian.' At this stage it never dawned on me that he had been killed by his own. So people were coming into the house and I was questioning them, 'Did you see Peter? What was he involved with, what was he doing?

Who killed him?' And nobody would give me any answers. I think everybody in Unity Flats was as confused as I was. People just thought it was sectarian.

He was shot for informing. The Provos shot him for that reason. They kept denying it and denying it, but in myself I knew they did kill him. People were talking about you, and saying, 'Her husband was shot for informing.' To be an informer is such an awful, awful thing in Catholic society and Irish society. To be an informer is the lowest of the low.

When his body was still in the house, they'd came and told me that he was killed on active service. That is what they told me and I was thinking, 'Highfield [a Loyalist area in Belfast]? This doesn't add up! It's not right!' But I said, 'OK, if he was killed on active service, then give him a military funeral.' They said, 'No, you've got four children. If you give him a military funeral you won't get any insurance money.' I said, 'I don't care about the insurance money, if he died that way he should be buried that way.' 'Oh no, we couldn't do that.' They knew they'd killed him and they couldn't give him a military funeral. I knew too, then, but you couldn't prove it.

I went to my brother's house in that year, in 1981. I went over to stay with him for a while. I was going to go to England for about six weeks and see if I liked it. So I went over anyway, but when I was there, it came out in the newspapers. Some journalist had uncovered the story – the police had probably given them the story – to say that Peter was a double agent. He had been selling information to the police, getting money from the IRA to give the police information, and then the police had finally hooked him in, somewhere along the line.

I don't know how they blackmailed him or how they scared him into giving them the information. I always believed that he thought, somehow or other, what he was doing was not wrong, as long as he was getting a lot of information to this one policeman, that it was OK. The IRA knew that he was doing it, like! They knew he was getting information to this policeman, but the policeman, somehow or other, was uncovered by the police. They found out that this policeman was selling information and then they knew obviously that Peter was the one that was getting it. So they must have leaked it out to the Provos that Peter was giving information.

I used to go up to the Sinn Fein centre on the Falls Road and asked them over and over did they kill him, and they kept saying no. Then it came out in the paper when I was away. The people that you thought were your friends were saying things like, 'She must have got a lot of money out of it! She must have knew he was doing it.' But I didn't. I wouldn't be working in the school cleaning for three hours a day if I was getting that sort of money.

What they said in the paper was that the policeman who was involved with Peter was suspended and has now left the country. The police never gave his name because he has relatives still living in Northern Ireland. But I've got relatives here, too. I had four children to bring up. Yet they printed their names, and they printed my husband's name.

People wanted to hear the story, maybe the gory details, but not about how you were coping or dealing with it. I felt I was always being watched. I was so angry with Peter that he would get that deeply involved with something and put his life at risk and leave me with four children. That made me really angry. My sister was like a building block for me. I looked at how she was, and she was guilty. She wasn't guilty of anything, but she felt this real sense of guilt, that feeling that she shouldn't have opened the door that night.

But I was just angry that he had done this quite deliberately and got himself into this situation that he could not get himself out of. And also, that he never told me about it. He'd left that night to go out with this fella and knew that he wasn't going to come back. He must have known he wasn't going to come back.

My family was very supportive. I think they were afraid of me dying because Maureen had died, and it was the similar circumstances again. So the one thing I didn't take was any tranquillisers or sleeping tablets. I just said no, that I wasn't taking any. I'd rather go through it and make it feel real, so it will maybe go away quicker.

My daughter was only a year and a half. If I hadn't had her, I don't know how I would have got through it, for she just demanded attention. You still had to go through the same routine – bring them to school in the morning, make lunches, clean the house.

The children were in bed that morning when the police came, so they heard the policeman telling me that Peter was dead. I don't know what happened to them after that. I should have went up and sat with them. I think they were in a bad state, crying and all. My eldest son was ten, the wee girl was nine, and the next one was seven. People came and took them away, and I kept saying, 'I want them in the house! I don't want them staying in other people's houses!'

After a funeral it's an awful feeling when everybody goes away, and you were sitting there at nights on your own, thinking about all things. It was wee small things like going up to the bathroom and using a bar of soap. He had washed his hands on that bar of soap three days ago, and the bar of soap is still sitting there, and he's not you know. Small things like that were big shocks. The wee things are the worst things. Christmas time was really hard. Peter and I had stuff left away for the kids and we were paying it off weekly. But people thought we'd money, and thought I'd be out buying the best of stuff if your husband was a top informer.

I was thirty at that time and I felt like my life was over. This was it! This was going to be me for the rest of my life, four kids and this flat and that would be it. I was too old to make any sort of changes with my life and that was very depressing.

But then I started going out a lot. And I was out this night, and I met this fella. He asked me to go out with him and he totally pursued me. He kept coming to the house and sending me letters, so I started to go out with him. But my husband's family didn't like that. So there was the pressure of wanting to do it, and not wanting to do it, and how to deal with all this. I'd been going out with Peter since I was about seventeen. So all them years with one person, I just hadn't a clue about how to behave any more.

Then I began to get sick myself. I began to get very bad pains in my stomach and I used to wake up at nights in real agony, with very bad pain. I went to the doctor and he said it was ulcers. So he gave me tablets, like my sister had got for her ulcers. The pain was really bad and it went on for years and years. I finally had to go into hospital and get gallstones out, and then I had to get my gall bladder removed.

The last time I was in the hospital I had a really big operation on my stomach, down the front of my stomach. This was about 1988 and it was for a blockage of the stomach. I couldn't eat. If I ate I was sick, so they took me in and put me through an operation.

After my husband's death, my stomach was constantly tight all the time. I was always very aware that people were judging me, because I've heard people saying, 'Oh I've seen her going out and she always has something new on her.' I've had these clothes for years, it was just that before, when I was out with my husband I wasn't a person in view then. But now, because I'm the topic of conversation, people look at you and see what you are doing. I used to sneak out the other way when I was in Unity Flats, so that the neighbours wouldn't see you. It was awful.

So then I moved. I bought a house in 1982 in Banning Street. But no matter where you went when people heard the name 'Valente' and because it is such an unusual name, I knew they were going to say, 'Are you anything to that fella that was killed?' After he was killed there were another two fellas shot for informing. The strange thing was that people never said anything to me or my family about Peter being an informer, or put us out of the area. They did that with a lot of people. They told you to get out or were very nasty to you. There was never any of that stuff.

Peter's brother was still in jail on the dirty protest at the time and when it came out in the newspapers they (the Provos) went up to the jail to see Jim to explain to him why they killed his brother. They told him they had tapes, if he wanted to listen to them, or if I wanted to listen to the tapes. So Jim got in touch with me and asked me did I want to and I said, 'No, I'm not going to listen to tapes for them'uns to explain to me why they killed my husband.' The thought that they had his voice on tape saying what he'd done and they wanted me to listen to it – it was awful.

At the inquest the whole circumstance of how he died was terrible. They drove him down from the Falls Road, it must have been German Hill. And they drove him down in a car down the Springfield Road to Highfield and walked him up an entry at Highfield. Then they shot him in the back of his head. His eyes were shut tight and when he fell, they shot him. So he had a bullet hole here. I think they took him to Highfield to try to make it look like a sectarian murder. I could never understand that.

Somebody said to me afterwards – I don't know who it was because I heard that many stories – that Peter had said to them, 'Don't let my family know what happened. Don't let my family know why you shot me.' They said, 'OK, we'll make it look like a sectarian murder.' And he had agreed to that. Usually they just dump informers' bodies outside Belfast on the main road.

A woman told the inquest that her wee boy had been delivering *Telegraph*s [newspapers] and he had seen the body in the entry, but thought it was a drunk man and he went and got her and she came out. She said to me it was like a bundle of rags lying there, and it wasn't until she looked close that she realised that it was a man's body lying in an entry. That was awful, like, just to put him in an entry and kill him.

The compensation thing was a real farce. I never thought of going to a solicitor because I had Peter insured enough to cover the funeral expenses and to get us over that Christmas. I was always very independent anyway, as I always worked and always relied on my own resources, although he was a good husband. He worked all the time and we were never short of money. He was in a well-paid job. When the solicitor sent for me I went down and gave him all the details of Peter and how he was shot and how many kids I had, I got the widow's benefit for me and four kids.

When the claim came through he told me that they'd offered me £4,000 and £500 for each child. I said OK. But at the same time I was thinking, 'A lot of people get hundreds of thousands!' At that time there was someone selling a house in Spamount Street for £4,000. So I said I'm going to take that £4,000 and buy this house. That is what I did. And it got me out of Unity Flats, and now I've my own house.

It was my own house and there were no memories of Peter in it. I used to have these dreams that Peter had come back and he'd come back to Spamount Street. I still have these dreams that he isn't dead, it wasn't his body that was found, it was just someone who looked like him and he's back. And then because I had moved house, I had got myself a job, and I was going with this fella and the kids were getting a bit older, he used to come back. And I'd go, 'I don't want you back!' There is no room in my life left for him, my life has changed too much.

And then there are other times I still dream about him, and say, 'This is good, he is back and he's alive, but I don't love him the way I did then. That's all changed!' I had dreams some nights that I'm lying in bed and I can feel this person getting into bed beside me and I can actually feel him putting his arms around me. I know it's Peter, and I'm going, 'Oh, this is terrible, this is terrible!' And I'm trying to wake myself up, trying to get to the top of water, and when you get to the top you are awake. I only took my wedding ring off after about seven or eight years. I still wear the engagement ring. I still haven't got round to taking that off completely.

In 1990, my daughter's boyfriend was killed. And the strange thing is that that affected me more than all the rest. It was because I seen him and he'd been in the house. My daughter lived next door to me, and him and her lived together with her wee baby. I really liked him. His family had had terrible trouble, terrible things happened to his family in the Troubles as well. Something like two aunts and two uncles were killed when a Saracen truck hit their car and killed the whole family.

He was sitting in the house on his own and I heard the bangs. My daughter and my sister-in-law were in my house. I heard a big Bang! Bang! Bang! But it sounded like someone kicking a tin. He came up the hall, and he was the type that was always having accidents. And I looked and said, 'What happened to you?' He had his hand up and he was all dazed and shocked and he said,

'They've shot me, they've shot me!' And then the blood started pumping out of his mouth, and the walls were covered in it.

I just grabbed him, opened the living room door, and put him into the living room, never said to anyone what was happening, and got on to the phone right away and rang for an ambulance. When I was on the phone, I could hear my daughter screaming in the living room and she run out by me. By this time the house was filled with people. He was sitting in the chair, and now and again I'd look in, and I'd go, 'I'm not going in to talk to him, I can't talk to him, I can't cope with this!' He was bleeding really badly. People came in and tried to give him first aid.

It seemed to take ages for the ambulance to come. When we walked into his house you could smell the gun shot, the cordite and you could smell it in the living room. You could see where they had shot him; the bullets had come right through the settee. They put him into the ambulance and my son Sean said he'd go with him. When they got him into the ambulance, they began cutting up his jumper, and he says to them, 'Don't be cutting that jumper! Marie bought me that jumper today! Don't be cutting that jumper or she'll go crazy if you cut this jumper off me!' It was only when they got it open that they realised it was his chest that was injured – it was like an artery, so every time his heart pumped, the blood just came out of his mouth.

So when he got to hospital Sean rang to say that he was going to be all right. The hospital said he would be OK. But then they discovered it was a main artery, and before they got him down to theatre he had died. He had bled to death.

It was a purely sectarian murder. He didn't do anything, he wasn't involved in anything. He was a bit of a hood, like. He was one of these people who would have robbed Dick to pay Paul, and he was a gambler and enjoyed drinking – just a normal twenty-one year old. When the police came they interviewed all of us and they said, 'Do you think it might have been a punishment shooting?' I said, 'A punishment shooting is when they take you out and shoot you in the legs. They don't come into your living room and shoot you in the chest, so it definitely wasn't a punishment shooting.'

So they interviewed every one of us and assured us they would definitely get somebody for the murder. Strangely enough the policeman that came out was the same policeman that came to my door to tell me my husband was dead. He couldn't believe it himself. He kept saying, 'I can't believe it is the same family.' He remembered that really well.

The police were trying to say that it was an internal feud between the INLA and the IRA. I just knew it was the Loyalists but they denied killing him. It wasn't until about three weeks later that they killed a fella in Duncairn Gardens and it was the same gun that had been used to shoot Gary. The police never came out to say that to us to say, yes, it was UVF.

My daughter was saying to me after Gary had died, that after Jim Foggarty died and then his wife died and then her daddy died, my children naturally assumed because they were kids that I would die too. She said, 'I used to make Peter and Sean lie awake at nights until you went to bed. I used to listen down the stairs to hear if you were coughing or making a cup of tea or turning the fire off and then going to bed and then I used to go to sleep.' I never knew all this until she was telling me. She said, 'I couldn't sleep at nights until you'd gone to bed.' And she constantly worried that I was going to die, that something was going to happen to me.

Then, when it happened to her, she went to see a psychiatrist up in Lagan Valley Hospital and he wanted to talk to her about what had happened. She started telling about her daddy dying as well and he said to Marie, 'You will survive this because you have had very good building blocks. You've had your aunt, you've had your mother and you've seen that she has survived this.' So then she realised, yes, I am going to survive this and she has. She is married now and has another wee baby. She met a really nice fella and she is doing really well.

The effect it has on your life? It's had a really bad effect. I mean there are things I'd maybe be doing now, that I've achieved, that I wouldn't have done, only for all those things happening. And then there are things you wish had've stayed the same. You'd wish your husband was still here and that my sister and her husband were here. It just scars your whole family.

Whether those scars are better or worse, I don't know. I suppose it is how you deal with them. That's the difference. I'd probably still be living in Unity Flats and I'd still be working in the schools, cleaning the schools, whereas now I've got a job in the community centre and I went and done my GCSEs. I have a job now that I love and I'm going to Queen's University and I've also had a wee boy since Peter died, to that fella I was going with.

3   Serious Injury

This interview was conducted by Marie Smyth in 1994. The interviewee wishes to remain anonymous. He is a member of the Disabled Police Officers Association and he was injured whilst on duty when the car he was travelling in was the subject of a gun attack.

I'm a member of the Disabled Police Officers Association. And I received my injuries in June 1972. I was a full-time member of the Royal Ulster Constabulary (the RUC, the Northern Ireland Police Force) and I was serving in Andersonstown at the time. I was travelling home from Andersonstown in a private car with a companion after doing a day's duty. Both him and I were clad in civilian clothes. On the West-link (motorway), a car came along as if to overtake and when it drew level with us the occupants of the passenger's front seat and the passenger's rear seat opened up with what I know now to be an Armalite rifle and a Thompson sub-machine-gun. My companion and I were very seriously injured. The vehicle that the gunmen travelled in crashed on one side of the road after an impact with our vehicle, and our vehicle crashed on the left-hand side of the road. An ambulance came on to the scene fairly quickly. My companion and I were conveyed to the Royal Victoria Hospital. Although I was very seriously injured, I remember quite vividly walking with assistance from the car to the ambulance and at the hospital, walking from the ambulance into the hospital. I remember when they cut the clothing off me, and the weapon that I was carrying in a side holster, telling the nursing staff there not to touch the weapon as it was fully loaded and the policeman would come along and look after it. A short time later my wife, who is a nursing sister, came along to the hospital.

By this time I was in the theatre, they didn't want to keep me lying too long without further medical attention. I remember quite clearly telling the wife to go along and look after the family, that I would be allright. Memories of the incident then faded for quite some time. No doubt many serious injuries do, depending on whatever type of sedation was administered at the hospital.

As a result of my injuries I've very restricted movement in my right arm. My walking is impaired as a result of injuries to my left leg and I am a permanent epileptic. I permanently take medicine for epilepsy and since those injuries I have had quite a few *grand mals* and a lot more *petit mals* with the epilepsy. Restricted injuries to my right arm do impede me in a lot of ways and I have overcome it to a certain extent that I am now able to write quite well and to do most things though I would be a lot slower at it than I would normally have been. My eyesight is also affected. When I look down I have to be very careful when descending steps, stairs etc. Generally speaking, I am aware of these injuries most of the time and take certain measures myself that would maybe appear to others that my injuries wouldn't be as bad as what they are.

It is a subject I wouldn't bring up myself in conversation. I would be reluctant to. I'm that type of a person that would feel that maybe I would be giving them the impression that I was looking for something or that I was playing on my injuries. I would try to get on with the business as best I can but I know that there are certain areas of my life when I have to have somebody near me or somebody has to have access to me. Now at home, I wouldn't go into the bathroom and close the bathroom door in case I went into one of these fits. I do drive. That was only after a certain number of years when the doctor cleared me. I had to have a medical examination on that and then I took one of the *grand mals* and I was off the road for a while again but then I've got that cleared again. Those are areas of my life that have been affected.

I try to do a bit of fishing to sort of get me away, well I would always have to have somebody with me who knows the circumstances if I go for a day's fishing or something like that there. So I just can't go out on my own and I mean, I feel allright with certain distances and things like that there, but I just wouldn't say to the wife or the family, 'I'm away to such and such a place for the weekend.' I wouldn't venture things like that there, which I could have done before. It's only recently that I've sort of come to terms with this at all.

Now I'm a member of the committee this year in the Disabled Police Officers Association, but up until this year, I wouldn't have allowed myself that. I thought that I would have been more of a hindrance than a help. And at times I would feel that this is the case, they tell me that's not so. It is difficult just to say, you try to get on with life as best you can. It's hard just to recall when I am talking to you but there are areas in my life that are affected.

3. Uniform hat of the Royal Ulster Constabulary as worn in 1975. Photograph: Marie Smyth

I would see it in my family, one daughter in particular now if she saw me going quiet or something in the house there, she would say, 'Daddy are you all right?' I know that it affects her as one of these *grand mals* or *petit mals* or whatever of these comes on. And at some stage every day, due to medicine – I'm on Phenobarb you see – I would have to have my wee sleep. And that can be inconvenient at times you know, if you are down staying with friends you just decide you are going to sit down in the chair and have a sleep. It doesn't look normal you know. I do have to have that wee bit of respite every day.

Usually I can feel it coming on and get on with it. I try to make the best of mine too. The epilepsy was acquired just as a result of injuries. I'd two bullets went in here at the temple and right through the front. I have a plug as they call it in from here to here. And that gives me trouble from time to time too. Great credit to the people in the Royal Victoria Hospital who were able to do this you know. And this arm was so badly affected at that particular time that they thought I might lose it. They kept coming in and trying to puncture these fingers and said, 'Is there feeling here?' I mean the both bones were cut right through and there is a plate in there holding it together.

I'm very very fortunate that that medical team were there at that particular time you know, to look after me. As well as being an in-patient in the hospital for quite some time, I would still be attending the hospital on occasion yet for them to look at me. In fact the tablets I was on were Epanutin and they stopped working after twenty-odd years so they had to change me on to something else. And during the time they were changing me over there, they just can't take you off one set of tablets and put you on to another. They phase you off one and phase you on to another and they have me now on Tegratol which is a very good tablet, and they have got me stabilised again as it were.

So this is twenty-two years on we are talking about. That this is the type of treatment that I am still having. They did give me sort of light duties in the police for a period but then I was medically discharged. I think the police maybe possibly tried at one stage to do this for everybody but then the injuries were getting so many that they became top heavy with people like us and couldn't facilitate us at that particular time. Again my pension sort of ceased and I'm on another pension. Now the financial compensation claims that some of them get! Knowing now that the claim that I got, it was only a pittance at that particular time, you know! I had to rear five of a family on it and my wife had to look after me and keep me. I feel a bit sore about that. I mean, it wasn't the police at that particular time, it was the government and the people handling these issues.

I suppose you are always wise after an event but I feel that the people out there should have been more professional in their approach to us and sort of knowing what was in front of us. It seems that the claim that I got was saying, 'Sure, what will he need money for now anyway? He's written off!' I would have a bit of bitterness in that, and I'm not a bitter person as such, I get on with all types of people.

Unless somebody in the local police station knew and took an interest in welfare committees and things like that, these weren't so prevalent in those days. You just had to make the best of it you know. It wasn't easy. I was thirty-eight years of age.

I don't talk about it. I would be very conscious about it. There is also the post-cease-fire, the security aspect of it too, that would have been there. But not only the security aspect of it. I'd be very reluctant to discuss it with in-laws and, you know my own family. If they sort of did catch me on, I'd become embarrassed about it and I would say, 'Acht leave me alone, I'm allright' and get on with it. I know it's probably wrong of me to keep this here, this lump in my stomach or knot in my stomach. I am just the type of person that can't, that is one aspect of it the physical aspect of it, I've tried to get on and get back to my fishing and I've tried to do a bit of work with regards to the DPOA and get on with that in that area of it allright.

This area that we are talking now is different for me. It is more difficult for me. I never was an outgoing person in any case but if that was the case before this happened, it seems to be more so. This is just that ball or knot in the stomach has got bigger as a result of this. I would get to the stage when I would just say, 'That's enough.' It would build up in me I would just dry up. There would be a bit of probably fear there. I know there's a fear. It's something that I have lived with and I would say there's some aspects of this that I didn't even discuss with my own wife. And whether I didn't discuss it with her or not is, I'm saying to myself, 'Would she understand?' And there is something else saying to me, 'Yes, she will understand. She was a nurse, she should know, have an idea about this'. But still it just remains there you know.

I wouldn't be the first person to go into a room when there is sort of strange company, and just go over and make myself known to them. I would stand back, and then when I am standing back, I'm saying to myself, 'I'm sure they think he's an odd ball. Why is everybody else talking and he's not talking?' And this hurts me too. I would like to be able to go and say 'Oh I'm John and it's a great night.' But it just doesn't come like that to me.

I had a *grand mal*. I suppose possibly two years ago. I was in Ballyclare one day, and I had to be taken to the Moyle Hospital in Larne and went through that whole experience in that *grand mal*. And that was a very traumatic experience to me, to go through that again, just relived that whole night. That was the most vivid one I've had. That was a very, very severe one as regards being physically sore and that afterwards. When you take a *grand mal*, your muscles are very sore. For quite some time you are not the same person. It takes you quite a while getting over it.

I've had other little snatches here and there in nightmares and in dreams. I've wakened up with the sweat rolling off me and dreams – not about my own particular night but dreams of similar incidents – about bombs going off and me being there, or something else. That was twenty-two years after the incident. I would feel myself twitching going in to these *petit mals* you know. The muscles would twitch. If I was having a sleep, there, maybe in the afternoon, members of my family would see that certain parts of my body was twitching. But they don't leave you. You just sort of sleep that off and you are allright coming out the other end in an hour's time. Which is not the case with the *grand mal.* It is so horrendous. I couldn't really put it into words but I know myself how horrendous it was, you know.

I feel that confidence has a lot to do with it. And I have confidence in the doctors, the medical people, the medical profession that has dealt with me and confident now that these Tegratol tablets that they have got me on to has had the desired effect up to this moment in time.

At one stage I was asking myself questions, 'Is there any point in me being here?' In spite of the fact that I had a wife and a family and grandchildren. There was one stage that, 'Is there anything left for you John, would you not have been better taken out at that particular time?' And with my disabilities I felt that maybe I was hindering their lives as well, them having to bear in mind that I was there all the time, and was liable to go into one of these fits.

I am very, very, very jumpy. Like people have played pranks, come behind you and drop a tray or something like that there. I would be very, very angry if somebody did that. And I possibly didn't know what they were doing. It would affect me. If that happened at a function it would have serious effects on the rest of the night for me. I couldn't take much interest in the rest of the proceedings for quite some time after it. That is the only way I can sort of illustrate it to you.

I would be happy to get possibly six hours' sleep at night. Some nights I wouldn't get so much sleep and this could go on for three or four weeks. Now last night I had a tremendous night's sleep, you know. I did a bit of reading before I went down to sleep and I didn't waken this morning until half past seven. Well, that was about six hours, six and a half hours. But I need it. I would waken up early in the morning. If I wakened up at four o'clock or five o'clock in the morning, I'd have difficulty in most occasions to get over again. I might lie for maybe two hours before I could get over to sleep again. But most times, say, if I had only four hours' sleep. I would be better up trying to do something about the house. And it sounds strange maybe helping to make the dinner for that day at five o'clock in the morning, but I would be better doing that than wrestling about the bed trying to get to sleep.

There are areas of my memory that would be affected. Now numbers! Numbers I would be pretty good with, telephone numbers and things like that there. But names! Names would be a big problem with me. I wouldn't say I had a great memory.

Probably something on television would take me back, maybe not all the time you know. Or there would be people who had been seriously injured or murdered that I would hardly ever think about. Then there are people who have been murdered and I would remember those particular, whether or not they'd be in some way similar to my own, I don't know. But there are names that had been murdered that I would remember and others I would forget.

There have been so many both inside and outside the security forces. The chap who was injured along with me didn't come out the other end as well. In fact, I don't think he has ever socialised outside of his own home since then. At the moment he is in hospital in a geriatric ward for various reasons. His own condition, his wife and family not being able to look after him, he is epileptic as well and falls out of bed. And he falls out of chairs. I feel very guilty about that.

When I was able to go along and see him at his own home, I'd visit him fairly often. But seeing him in the condition did nothing for me. It made me very, very depressed and I stopped going to see him. And then I felt guilty about not going to see him.

It is only recently that I've been able to go along to the hospital to see him. He always refers to the particular station that we were in and the people that were serving at that particular time. And he leads a little bit on to the incident that happened to us and I can't handle that terribly well. As much as I would like to go and see him on a regular basis at the hospital, I have to be in a certain mood before I could say, 'Go on, you can take this today! Go on and do it.'

Well to be quite honest with you, to me it is a very uneasy peace. And I can't go out there yet as much as would like to, and have 100 per cent trust, feel 100 per cent safe. That is my feeling about it at the moment. And I would love to sit here and say to you today, I'll probably be allright you know. But I have children, grandchildren growing up, but not only for my own but for everybody out there you know. And there are certain areas that I certainly haven't gone to since I was injured, nor would I go to and feel safe in going to. It is difficult for me to try to mix, associate with everybody you know. Whether they be Catholic, Protestant, Hindu, Jew etc. I would like to be able to do that at all and I hope sometime in the near future would.

Well if there was an amnesty, one can never be sure that all the arms would be handed in. But I would like to have seen more of an effort being made. Because – let's face it – there is enough arms and ammunition around us to blow this little island out into the middle of the Lough. And I feel that there wasn't enough done in that area. Well no matter what type of organisation you set up or how close you knit the net, there is always going to be one or two slip through in any case. And circumstances alter cases and I would feel that there has been cases where the security forces have boobed. Maybe not intentionally, but boobed.

This barbaric sort of treatment has been handed out on both sides of the fence. I would rather see somebody in uniform coming, be it the army or police even though they have made these little blunders. Everybody is human as well – I would rather see them coming to deal with things than boys coming with cudgels or baseball bats or whatever. So that is an area that there has to be some development in.

Had I been able to engage those fellas that did the shooting at me I would have had no hesitancy at all in shooting them dead, standing over them and making sure they were dead. Because I felt that I was in the right. And I was in the right as a serving policeman. And they had no business coming along, whether I was a policeman or not – coming along an' opening up on me like they did. But if somebody come to me, say in six months' time, and says to me, 'John, we have the two guys up there that injured you that night, we have them up in a quarry some place, come on up now and shoot them there's a gun', I couldn't have done that. I couldn't have gone to bed and slept at night.

I have very, very good friends whom I have served with that have different religious persuasions than I. And I'd put 100 per cent trust in them. I know from serving in an area such as West Belfast that we had people up in there who were very caring people. And just to relate some instance after funerals, a lot of yobs that come out after funerals and stoned the police station and broke the windows and people who were living round that station came out and brushed up the street and helped us to clean up the station. And we had a great relationship with most people in areas like that. I know that would be the case today, but how do you deal with these other thugs? And this is what we are getting at.

And I see the position regarding those in jail and having been properly convicted. They never were any use to our society whilst they were in jail. And does having served three years in jail and letting them out, does it make them any better? Would they be any better to our society? And they have facilities in there to avail of. They can get on with their studies. And they are provided with a fairly good facility in there. In fact there was some of them far worse off before they went into jail.

4   Living with the Aftermath

This female former prison officer is in her forties and from a rural area in Northern Ireland. She was the subject of a gun and grenade attack in 1979 whilst coming off duty. She wishes to remain anonymous and was interviewed with her sister and brother-in-law, who participated in the interview. (Their words are shown in italics.) The interview took place in her home.

In 1972 I saw the advert in the paper. I knew of one prison officer. Her cousin lived next door, so I thought I'd try it. I worked for a long time. I was in hospital in March. It was a professor in the Royal who operated on me. It was a woman's complaint. He told me I'd have to have a month off, that I wasn't so good. But I decided I'd go back to my work. I got out on the Friday and went to the doctor on the Saturday and signed myself off and went in to work on the Monday.

And then it came to April. I'm on the shops in the prison and I went to the cash and carry that day. This was 1979. [Another female prison officer] was there and I drove her car up that morning. She didn't like driving up the Armagh Road.

[Sister]They all went out to the prison. There was four of them and as they were crossing the road they saw nothing. They were actually checking their pay. They were going over to have a meal in the Wagon Wheel.

[The interviewee] said she thought she heard a noise, and she felt the pain in her finger. She slid straight down to the ground. She said it was like going in slow motion. And when she went down to the ground the other girl she went to sit up. And she says, 'They're shooting.' [The interviewee] says, 'Lie down, they'll think we're dead' and the other girl [the other female prison officer], she was standing up ... And they threw the grenade ...

They threw the grenade at her and blew the whole side out of her and she was killed. The other girl got it in her foot. But the girl that she told to lie down she got it in her legs. [The interviewee] was shot through the breasts. And when she landed on the ground she damaged her whole back.

42

The authorities came along and they brought people. The ambulance came and [the interviewee] got word to one of the men to not let the police go and tell mammy for it'd kill her. They got her on to the stretcher. First of all they brought her to Armagh Hospital and they saw how badly she was and then they took her to Craigavon.

A friend of ours works in the telephone exchange. She phoned me and told me that there were prison officers shot at Armagh but not to worry that [the interviewee] wasn't one of them. I says to mammy, 'She couldn't be one of them for she had went to the cash and carry that morning.' [Telephone operator] says, 'I got the names.' And I says, 'Is one of the names [a second female prison officer]?' She says, 'Yes.' I says, 'Oh my goodness! Her mammy and daddy are in Belfast.' So I lifted the phone and phoned her father and I says to him '[The second female prison officer] has been shot. Is it all right if I go over to Craigavon Hospital, she'll have somebody that she knows. I'll go over and I'll see her.' His car wasn't on the road at the time. He had to get the lend of a car.

I was at the Craigavon Hospital and I went in to see [the second female prison officer] but they wouldn't let me see her. She was going to theatre. I never passed any remarks on anybody and I says, 'It's taking her family an awful lot of time coming from Belfast.' But I'd given my word to stay and I didn't want to leave. I says, 'I'm going to phone mammy and tell her that we'll go up and pick [the interviewee] up and I'll bring home something for the tea.'

When I rang home to tell mammy the Reverend answered the phone. I knew his voice immediately and I said, 'What are you doing there?' And he said 'I have good news and bad news for you.' I said, 'Oh my God [the interviewee]'s shot!' 'Yes,' he says, 'she is.' And I said, 'There's one of them dead, it's [the interviewee!]' He said, 'No, she's not dead.' And he said, 'Don't put the phone down, I have a policeman over there looking for you.' I said, 'There's no policeman here.'

I didn't care if they were looking for me or not. I run out and I told my husband. He got out of the car and he was holding on to it. When I came back later he was still standing in the same way. He didn't seem to be able to move with the shock.

I went in and they said to me, 'Come on in here and have a wee cup of tea.' And I said, 'This is no time for having tea!' And the policeman said, 'Well, I haven't had a bite since breakfast time.' I said, 'Well, when I've seen [the interviewee] then you can have your tea!' I still didn't believe that she wasn't dead. So they took me away down to this place and they dressed me all in white. When I looked at her, God bless us! The only white part of her was the white of her eyes and her teeth.

4. Disabled prison officer injured in 1979. This photograph was taken in her home in December 1998. Photograph: *Sunday Life*

She was completely black. When she looked at me, she started to cry. She since told me she thought she was in heaven.

I met with the doctor. He was a coloured man. He was nice. He said only she was a plump lady she would not be here because the bullet passed a knife edge from her heart. I was coming back from seeing [the interviewee] and they'd given me a white bag with 'patient's property' written on it. I was lost. And who did I meet only [the telephone operator] who had phoned me. She came along and says, 'Don't take that bag home to your mother for it'll kill her!' At the bottom of the bag was blood. She says, 'I'll take that and get rid of that for you.'

When I got home, mammy was sitting and the kitchen was full of people and the Reverend was still there. Poor mammy says, 'Daughter, when I saw the man and woman I thought they were missionaries that were here for their tea.' The two police had arrived in plain clothes with the Reverend. Anyway, mammy she says to me, 'Tell me the truth!' And I told her exactly what I had left. She says, 'I couldn't go the night, love. I'll stay here and mind the boys, you go back.' I went back to the hospital and stayed with her a long time. She drifted in and out of consciousness. Then in time, they let her out of the intensive care.

You couldn't have got near the bed for flowers. She had a marvellous policeman to look after her who has since become a good friend of the family. He was on guard duty with [the interviewee]. She was guarded night and day. I could go home and do a turn in the house and rest a minute with mammy when I knew he was there.

In a short space of time, I couldn't tell you how long, they came back into the hospital again – this woman at night-time. She said she had lost her handbag. She had been visiting somebody in the hospital. The nurse had went away to get her a painkilling injection. [The second female prison officer] was in a bed beside her. It was a ward for two people and she was asleep. And the policeman – one of them had gone down to get something to eat in the canteen and the policewoman, she was in the toilet.

The woman came in through the door and [the interviewee] let a scream out of her. [The interviewee] knew her. An ex-prisoner who was, we take it, gathering information as to where they were and how they were. The staff in the hospital apprehended her. They moved [the interviewee] then from where the females were up to where the men were.

They operated on my chest five times. It kept going bad inside ...

[Sister] And turning black.

Then they'd take more off it and then they were going to put me in the decompression chamber. The surgeon was very angry that it wouldn't heal.

[Sister] They sent her home.

He was angry because he said I couldn't settle. And he said it was never going to heal. Whenever I got out of bed I couldn't walk. I'd walk three chairs and have to sit down until the pain eased and then I could walk three more chairs. That's how I got about. This Thursday he'd come and he said, 'I'm going to take a chance and I'm going to send you home but I want to see you every day.' The stitches were pulled out of my breast, so I got home. I didn't even wait for my clothes. I didn't even wait for the police. When I got home my sister made a sling and tied it round my neck and it healed through time.

How did you feel after you realised what had happened?

I remember I asked the doctor, 'What about [the second female prison officer]?' And he said, 'She has a bad leg, but she's all right.' And I said, 'What about [the third female prison officer]?' And he said, 'We're discharging her. She's going home, she's all right.' And I said, 'What about [the first female prison officer]?' And he said, 'She's sleeping, she's all right. She's sleeping peacefully.' Whenever I come round, I don't know when it was they told me that she was dead. In the hospital, you didn't get a chance to really think about what has happened, because we had a policeman and a policewoman there with us the whole time. And if you got down, or if you were thinking they cheered you up. You never got thinking, 'This has happened!'

When did it come home to you that it had happened?

When I was in the market ...

[Sister] She went to Portadown market the first week she got out. And a woman says, 'I thought you were in the hospital, I thought you were shot in Armagh.' She couldn't get out of the market quick enough.

I went into delayed shock and then my nerve broke ...

[Brother-in-law] You were in a shop in Armagh and somebody tapped you on the shoulder and said, 'We're not finished with you!' Isn't that right?

Just ... I couldn't cope ... I turned then. The psychiatrist gave me tablets. And I used to sleep all day and be awake at night. I turned night into day. When they were getting up, I lay down.

[Brother-in-law] Many a time she calls me to open the window to let the smell of the bomb out.

[Sister] They were pumping tablets into her called Halcium. They were desperate tablets, they were driving her out of her mind. I knew she was taking too many of them – but she wasn't overdoing what Craigavon had told her to take. This night, she was in an awful way and I said ...

Tell her the truth.

[Sister] She went for me with a knife. I said, 'This can't be.' There was nobody I knew. I didn't know any psychiatrists for they were people we never had any occasion to need. I said, 'What in God's name am I going to do?' We went to a psychiatrist privately. She still was taking

many of the tablets, three of them three times a day and maybe an extra one or two at night.

What did [the private psychiatrist] do? He gave her seven tablets for one week. One tablet a day. He said to her, 'If you don't quit them, you'll no longer see, for one of the side effects of them is blindness.' Then the bother starts. Imagine nine to ten tablets a day reduced to one a day, seven a week.

She even tried to buy them privately but couldn't because they were very dangerous drugs. She used to get mad and she used to phone him up and call him everything on the phone. You know what he used to say? 'That has done her good, she's got rid of it!' When she had finished talking to him she would have fell into an exhausted sleep. That man was a godsend to us. And that man saved her eyesight.

What do you remember about that whole period?

It was hard going now. I can remember feeling very angry. You'd just love to hurt somebody as much as you're hurting.

Did you have to see doctors or psychiatrists in connection with compensation?

They sent me to many doctors; my nose was affected and my ears were affected and I had to have operations for them.

[Sister] She has had to return to various hospitals many times. She had surgery on her ear and nose in Craigavon and in the Royal for her surgery on her eyes. And she still needs further surgery on her eyes. When she is in hospital, I stayed with her even at night. She is terrified and is never left on her own. Back pain and leg pain are constant companions. And she has been a diabetic for eleven years.

The compensation was … I went one day – they wouldn't let me into the courtroom. They said I wasn't to go in but I couldn't take it being in that wee room. The solicitor, he came and said, 'I want you to come with me.' I said, 'Where are we going?' And he said, 'Just for a wee minute, you'll only be a minute.' He didn't tell me. I was brought into this room and it was all full of men but most of them were doctors.

The family doctor came over and he started to unbutton my blouse. I was buttoning it up and yet nobody said to me that this was a judge's chamber and we're going to look. He said I might have to go to the judge's chambers and I said I wasn't going. I wasn't going to strip off in front of anybody that did photographs. I said, 'I worked in the prison and you wouldn't have been allowed to have done that with a murderer what youse are trying to do to me and I'm not going.' But anyway they got the blouse off me and they got looking at me.

I come home from the court and I tell you I didn't know what was going on. It didn't make sense to me. I had told the solicitor in my own house in front of them I wasn't going in no judge's room to strip. But he came on the day of the court and he said '[Interviewee], will you come with me?' My sister gave me tablets and I got up and I said, '[Sister], will you get the solicitor on the phone?' And she says, 'What do you want him for?' I said, 'I'm going to tell him to take whatever they're offering. I don't want to go back there anymore. I don't want to have to think of the next fortnight and going back again.'

Then it came out on the Monday morning that I had been awarded so much damages. It was on the front of the paper and it was on the television. They had promised me my name or nothing would go in. There was people phoning me and people at the door. It was dreadful. That's how they compensated ...

[Sister] Don't forget the old man who was sitting on the case – the man that was representing you. He turned round and said there was nothing wrong with her. He said if she had lost a leg or an arm or an eye ... He asked me how much did we want for the claim and I said a hundred thousand, for she's injured. And he says, 'Not at all! If she got fifty, it would do her rightly!' He was an ignorant man. I'm sorry I didn't take him up for stripping her.

A prison officer who was off duty saw the incident of us being shot and was awarded £50,000. Yet I got £60,000 and I had to pay £1,500 to an accountant to represent me in court. As far as the Prison Service goes the only folk who have done anything for me are the Prison Officers Association, whose chairman is Mr Finlay Spratt – the only person who has even cared.

How has the whole thing left you now?

It's just like living a nightmare that's the only way I can put it to you. It's just living a nightmare every day.

[Sister] It's just existing.

[Brother-in-law] She can't walk or nothing.

[Sister] And she would dearly, dearly love a holiday. We haven't had a holiday. We went to Donegal. We went on a Saturday and we had to come back home on a Monday. She wasn't able to sleep in the bed. In our house there's the hoist to pull her up and there was none of those things and her chair has a recliner which goes back out.

[Sister] Now she has taken diabetes out of it and she has a cataract on her eyes. They gave us an amount at the time she was shot but you see where it has gone to and what good is it?

What about emotionally, how are you?

[Brother-in-law] Just can't leave her.
   [Sister] She is never left.
   [Brother-in-law] If I was going to town here I would take her with me for she thinks there is something going to happen me. If anything happened me then she'd be stuck for [her sister] wouldn't be fit.
   It's just a living nightmare.
   [Brother-in-law] So she comes with us.
   But then I can only stay in the shop a very minimum time, two minutes at the most ...

Do you get panic attacks?

Yes, and short of breath. And palpitations, I'm on that many tablets and I get so tired but yet I don't sleep, and nightmares.

Are the nightmares related to what's happened to you?

They all have come from that, they say.

And you're still having the panic attacks?

I have flashbacks.

And how often would you have panic attacks now?

Oh, it never changes. You can't say when you would have it or when you wouldn't have it. It just happens. If the dog would go missing or if anything happens out of the ordinary I can't cope with it. That's just the way it is. If everything is smooth, I'm all right but if anything happens out of the usual ...
   [The interviewee] is living for the day, with God's help, she'll never see. And she's waiting for them to come back again. I think it all stems back to the woman coming into the hospital and the woman in Armagh tapping her on the shoulder.

Do you feel scared that your life is still at risk?

I only wish that when they do it they do it right.

You're scared all the time that they're going to come back?

[Sister] She is searching for faces in the crowd. It doesn't alone affect her, it affects us all.
   [Brother-in-law] It affects the whole lot of us and I get angry.

[Sister] There's times when you're talking away to [the interviewee] and she doesn't even answer us. She gets awful silent and I don't like it, this last while.

Do you think you're a bit depressed?

[Interviewee nods]
   [Brother-in-law] Oh, yes very much.

None of the officials come?

No.

And how do you feel about that?

Hurt and angry that they should do that to me. I tried to explain to them not to be sending me flowers at Christmas because I always bought mammy flowers at Christmas. And I'm not a flowery person, but she was. It always reminded me of that. I miss mammy enough without flowers coming in to remind me. There are other things besides flowers. There was a whole row because the authorities thought I'd been dead for ten years. And then they came here and my sister says 'I feel like scalding you, youse have hurt her that much.' And they said that they'd be back. That was years ago. Then two men come and they said they'll get them to come but nobody come.

5   Taking Up Arms

Lawrence McKeown was interviewed in April 1997 in Ballymurphy, West Belfast. He is a former member of the IRA, who was involved in the hunger strike in 1982 in which ten men died.

I lived out in the country outside Randalstown so it was fairly quiet. I would have had an upbringing that was in a neighbourhood that was mixed. There was absolutely no sectarian element at that stage. Randalstown was seen as predominantly Protestant yet Catholics owned 50 per cent of premises.

I think it was after the formation of the UDR. A number of ones we drank with were suddenly in the UDR, and coming home at night, getting stopped by them, and then the ridiculous thing of them asking you your name, which, one night, when it first happened, turned into a laugh from ourselves in the car. But we seen fairly quickly that the ones who were asking it weren't seeing it as a laugh. I felt physically afraid of some areas or if you were stopped at night by the UDR you were very much conscious that this was like a Protestant Loyalist force. You had things like UDA in Randalstown and they became much more physical, so you would have felt under threat.

Patterns would have changed. We stopped drinking in Randalstown. You would have changed your route coming back from different places. You became very much aware what were safe areas.

I had thought about it. I was singing these [Republican] songs and talking and discussing what was going on about our defence and at the same time not playing any active part. So, I came to the decision to join the IRA, but it was a long thought out one and the process of getting into it was also a long one.

It was about a couple of months later that someone approached me one night. They had created a situation where I was with them and they said they had heard I was interested in joining the IRA and that the IRA at that time was interested in forming a unit in the area I lived in. I said I definitely was, and that took a procedure which took probably seven to eight months, to the point where I

5. Lawrence McKeown, former IRA prisoner, who joined the hunger strike in Northern Ireland in 1982. Family photograph

was getting exasperated, thinking that somebody had forgotten about me, that I wasn't moving ahead.

But then I was taken in and asked again by others in a more formal situation had I thought it out and was I aware of the consequences and to rethink my position, the fears of imprisonment, or being shot or killed or whatever. I said that I had thought of a lot of those issues that they had raised, that I didn't think I was going to change my mind. So, they said to give it some more thought but I didn't change my mind. Shortly after that I ended up in the IRA.

Whenever I became active in the IRA the operations carried out were always kept outside of the area so it wasn't too difficult to get out of the house to do things. I was seventeen at the time. After one operation where a car had to be hijacked, I had to then drive it to go down the road to pick up a bomb and bring it back up again. So, to go down the road I had to take the mask off and I didn't know at the time that the car had been seen getting hijacked. So, there was this crowd of people seen me and one of them knew me from school.

When the bomb went off in Randalstown my name started to be mentioned in a bar, so there was a lot of discussion about what we should do. I went home and my parents were out. I didn't know where they were – they were actually in a neighbour's house – but I saw another neighbour and I called her aside and said that I had to leave, that I was involved in that last bomb explosion in Randalstown and apparently I had been spotted and my name was out. I suppose it was a bit of a rush once the decision was taken. We were more aware of getting out immediately. So, I left and stayed round Toomebridge that night and next day was moved over the border into Monaghan.

It often seems very scary, but bombs, until they're primed, you can practically do anything with them so it's not as if you're sort of sitting waiting for something constantly to go off. Right enough, in those days the timing mechanisms were much more crude therefore liable to accidentally being put off. But if you were anyway careful at all you could totally reduce that. I suppose there's more of an acceleration, there's adrenaline once you're doing anything. I think anybody, should they be British soldiers or whatever else, once the operation is happening you're powered on by something that doesn't normally sort of propel you.

In 1973 or 1974, it would have been a fairly loose chain of command that I would have been coming into contact with. I mean, you certainly had your immediate superiors. There would have been infrequent meetings with them and the meetings would have been fairly informal. People got to know one another and each one had a role to do but there was a fair degree of independence.

Shortly after that I contacted my family and met with my mother and sister down in Monaghan, which was strained. I suppose she was concerned how I was and what was happening. The whole relationship I had with her afterward – she never really condemned me for what I was doing. I think my father would have been more disappointed. I had met him briefly, we only spent a couple of weeks together, but it was a fairly strained. I know he didn't agree with my politics or what I had done.

You ended up you had no money, you were staying in people's houses who were actually just keeping you. You were unsettled being there, you preferred to be in the North. Any romantic notions about being on the run very quickly disappeared. The contact with the unit stopped as soon as I left but it didn't stop with the IRA because they always had a structure in Monaghan and a structure which was tied in with people who were on the run, that was maintained.

I argued for an attack upon, well it could have been the British Army, RUC, UDR or whatever. It would be like a military patrol and it ended up I was on it myself. It was a July night it happened on, finally.

The attack was on an RUC Land Rover – one policeman was injured very slightly. But it was fairly close to even my own home. And then I was out of the house after that. Anyway, one night I ended up coming back to the house, it was on a Sunday night and the next morning it was raided. I was arrested and taken to Castlereagh, interrogated and charged with attempted murder and causing explosions previously.

I suppose Castlereagh seemed a bit more scary than being taken into Antrim or Ballymena, which might have been the norm in the past. I feared more physical interrogation which I think was more psychological than just sort of constant interviewing and changing and shouting a load of abuse.

I've often wondered, if I had made a verbal statement would it have been better for me? If there had been physical abuse, it might have shook me out of it. I feel my fight was down by that time. I think in terms of emotion, or psychologically, it meant that by the time I went into the barracks I was ready. On the third day of questioning I was charged, so from when I went in it was fairly constant. There would have been a bit of a break, meals, changing from ones to the others. I got to sleep at night. You were allowed time to sleep. The place was very warm, and because of what you are mentally going through at the time, I'm not sure you sleep much – or you sleep in a sort of exhaustion.

They wanted me to make a statement and name others, but I wouldn't. Once I actually made the statement, which was fairly brief, I wasn't saying anything and was happy about sitting saying nothing. There was no way I was mentioning anybody else or any weapons or explosives or anything. Maybe because I was now in the barrack for three days its newness or the uncertainty was starting to go. It was a relief to get out of Castlereagh. The only regret I had at that time was why I had made a statement.

I was taken to Antrim Courthouse to be charged then back to Crumlin Road. You are held in B Wing overnight. At that time the [political] status had been taken away so there was a mixture of Republicans and Loyalists. There was trepidation as to what was going to happen, a lot of shouting from screws, banging of doors, particularly in B Wing. I was very much unsure about prison uniform. I started to see other ones out there in the yard, the numbers that were there and the way that they were talking and you were thinking, 'It's not too bad!' They were saying, 'You will just be held there tonight and moved over tomorrow.' The next day I was moved over to C Wing. The screws even seemed more relaxed and now you were with people and you were getting out into the canteen.

1976 was a very good summer and a lot of time was spent in the yard, where we would have been talking about outside. A period of reminiscing – what would be going on tonight, where would you have been going. There would have been politics talked. You were getting more into reading because you were held in cells. You were starting to get introduced to Republican literature and you were meeting people from other different areas. You were allowed three visits a week, half-hour visits. There were times there were hassles over strip searches, but by and large they weren't the worst. The screw didn't stand sort of totally opposite you, he would have walked up and down, it was only in later years it became worse in the Crum [Crumlin Road Jail].

Altogether I was on remand nine months then moved to the H-Blocks. H-1 was very regimented, very closed in, single storey, seemed to be a lot of rules. I was just there less than a month and moved back to the Crum. I think I was moved about two days before it. They took you there because it was handy to the Courthouse. The court lasted two days, it was just dragging out all this. Somebody in the army tactical had to say, 'Yes, this explosion actually happened.' It was that sort of evidence rather than eye-witnesses. So, it lasted one full day and the next morning and then

I was sentenced that morning before dinner-time for five counts of life. I got four hundred years. I was just relieved it was over.

You knew you were going to be sentenced, you knew you were going to be in the protest and you actually wanted to be down and be on it. The following day I was moved. They took you to reception and you were put in these cubicles and told to strip and put on the prison uniform. We said we weren't wearing the uniform. The van stopped at H-2 and I was told it was me which I didn't really want. I expected the worst. You expected to be beaten up going into the place. That had been fairly much the norm. I walked into the circle and you seem to stand out so starkly and dramatically because you are told to strip, strip totally naked and stand there in the middle of the circle. So you are standing there totally naked and everybody is walking about, the floors are being polished and the screws are walking about and they are shouting and roaring and at one stage a crowd gathered round and I thought I was going to get a beating but it didn't come.

I was taken down to C Wing totally naked. I would say, definitely those three days there were the loneliest days I have ever spent. I actually ended up totally isolated because there was nobody next door to you. The other prisoners weren't allowed to speak to you although some of them were able to shout in or one time I got cigarettes put in.

I was then moved to H-5. You were living in the cell at the time a lot more and you still just had a blanket. At times there was furniture in the cell. You had a bed in it, a chair, a locker, a table and big locker where the prison uniform just stayed in it. In the mornings they would come round and we were given breakfast in the cell. At the very start people were made to go out naked for their meals, but once the numbers built up they weren't allowed to go out. What you were given was a towel. You got a shower twice a week and they would give out basins of water to wash in or for shaving. Other ones didn't bother shaving, just grew beards. All the water you were getting, you had to wash your hair in it, wash your face, all the rest of it. It wasn't even warm so it was another reason people stopped shaving. Plus you also brushed out your cell. There was a bell in your cell so you could get out to the toilet, you also slopped out, so there was that movement. The rest of the time you were locked up.

It was never envisaged that it would go from no wash to what ended up as putting excreta on the walls. We weren't allowed out to the toilets, so then there was all the practical difficulties that that posed. Disinfectants were put in the windows. We smashed windows. Other people started smashing furniture and before you knew it you were left with two bits of sponge and the blankets and a po.

Because we had the radio, we were able to hear about people calling for emergency status. This brought a whole sort of new life to the place and you now felt you were being active, as opposed to just sitting there and being sort of a victim of events, rather than having some sort of control over them. The only time I ever felt bad times, was the period immediately after the first hunger strike when it became clear that the Brits weren't going to give anything.

The thing that used to particularly get me was the food. The food was terrible. It was small amounts and what was even worse was the pettiness, because they put it on the trolley to bring it out and I heard the screw saying, 'It's too warm for them, let it sit for a wee minute there!' And it would sit for twenty minutes until the grease was sitting hard on it. Also, the fears of wing shifts, knowing you were going to get beat up.

I never wanted to leave the protest, simply because it was right I should be there. There had always been talk about a hunger strike, simply because within Republican history, in prison hunger strike had always been the ultimate. The decision had always been to try and exhaust every other means first. At one time in 1980 it was thought we were going to get our own clothes, which really would have ended the protest because that was the major thing. The uniform was the badge of criminalisation. It was felt that most of that had been exhausted, in terms of outside protesting and media coverage, so it was then decided that there would be a hunger strike. People were asked to put forward their names but there was seven people selected for it.

I think there was a change once the hunger strike started. I suppose the screws and administration were wary of what was going to happen and so forth, and similarly, when the second hunger strike came round. 1979 was probably the worst year but I think by the time it came to 1980, some of the worst screws were shifted out of the Blocks. We still had a fairly hostile situation but we did not actually have physical assaults on the same scale.

I think my health was fairly sound, although I was about two stone underweight, as most people were. You were really white because you weren't out in the sun but in spite of all those factors, you were probably as healthy as people outside – a bit malnourished but other than that. But there was things you seen later on, coming out. Once we got exercise after the next hunger strike it was the first time out in the yard in years and one fella was running across and another one chasing him and the person's legs just gave out because the muscles just weren't used to running.

I put my name forward. I was young, I wasn't married and I didn't have children. I believed that it was right, that everything else had been exhausted. A lot of people can't understand the hunger strikes without realising the years that went before it, that you are totally incarcerated in a cell twenty-four hours a day – you are in those conditions and that's the battle on it. I was doing life imprisonment so it was like the future of my life. The first hunger strike had ended after fifty-three days and on the fiftieth day there had been another group of thirty people joined the hunger strike and I was one of them. So, that night there was all the talk about what was going to happen in the morning and all this sort of exhilaration.

First thing in the morning, the doors were opened and some NIO official threw in this leaflet. There was a discussion about this document and it had been agreed there was enough in this foggy language that would resolve it and move us out of that situation. But within a couple of days, because there was no movement at all and suspicion set in very quickly. It was apparent that the screws weren't thinking there was going to be any big change. We were sitting exactly as we had been prior to the ending of the hunger strike. We knew something was going badly wrong. I think that was the worst time I ever spent in jail.

Within three weeks we got word there was going to be another hunger strike. The strategy was going to be different this time. That was the only thing that lifted me out of a depression. My biggest feeling at the time was anger at what had happened with the first hunger strike. It went from exhilaration, probably to disappointment, and then anger that the whole thing could have been worked out. People were taken to that brink and the hunger strike people agreed to end the hunger strike on the basis of, 'Yes, there is agreement here', without stroking every T and dotting every I and that had been thrown in your face.

I was sure this time the hunger strike would not end until political status was complete – that these five demands were being agreed to – publicly agreed to. When Bobby Sands won the election there was absolute euphoria. We had, for a number of years, radios smuggled in, small crystal sets, which was an elaborate process. When the election results were coming in we were told no shouting out the doors or it would be known that we had got the news immediately and that we had radios. I can remember the results coming through and it went from a muffled yelp on one side of the wing to just an absolute uproar and you could just hear the camp exploding.

The second hunger strike started really slowly. There was very little in the papers about it. Winning the election just really took us from a low point but generally it was felt it was going to be at the end before attention is focused here. It took us to new heights of saying, 'Bobby is now elected.' Surely they couldn't turn round and let him die on an issue where he is saying he is a political prisoner, there's thirty-odd thousand people who voted him in as their MP and therefore, obviously regard him as a political prisoner, and a Member of Parliament at Westminster. Maybe there was a bit of naïveté in that because within a week or two you were saying, well, 'They are intending that all right.'

I suppose for the few days prior to it you were just listening to the radio and knew we would get the report down from the hospital about the various states Bobby was in. It had actually been the next morning before we heard, our wing didn't have a radio at that stage. Bobby died early in the morning, it was two o'clock or round about then, and we sort of figured something when the screws came in that morning. They were very, very quiet. Brendan Hughes came up to the door and said, 'Bobby's dead.'

I think that day the wing was just totally silent. You heard people speaking out the windows a bit but there was none of the general noise or commotion. Everyone was generally just subdued.

There had been four people on the hunger strike, Bobby, Frank, Patsy and Raymond, and it had never been clear what would happen if all four of them died or what would happen if even one died. I can remember going to Bik McFarlane and asking him why I still hadn't been put on the hunger strike – it might sound like egotism or something but it's not. It's like, there's a battle on and I want to be stuck in it here. By the time I joined it all four original hunger strikers had died. I joined it in June, the 29th of June.

My mental condition varied, you knew your blood was going to become clearer but as time went on a weakness impinges upon it – you just get weaker and weaker. But initially the only thing is feeling fairly cold because you were meant to drink only water.

You drank ten pints of water a day. It was cold water and at that time of the year the heating was off in the Blocks so coldness was the only thing I would have felt. You never really lose the appetite – the food you were getting was terrible, but because you knew you weren't going to eat anything you didn't have that same feeling of hunger. Yes you felt an emptiness in your stomach for the first few days and after that your stomach starts to shrink down. After the fortieth day, the eyes started to get fuzzy, you have double vision, and then you wake up blinking into them.

We were moved to the hospital after thirty days. We were still locked in the cells during the day in the hospital but you were allowed out in the evening for association. You were allowed out during the day for an hour's exercise. You would walk down slowly. People just don't sort of deplete immediately once they stop eating because they obviously have all them reserves and they are not going to do anything really strenuous. I was on it seventy days, but up until about sixty-five days I still would have got out of bed. By that stage you were literally just getting out of bed to sit in an armchair at the side. You weren't really walking anywhere. If you were walking anywhere somebody was assisting you, but you could put your arm around somebody's shoulder and you could walk that distance.

You start out from the position of … you hope it's going to end before you die. You do end up thinking, I could die here – but that changes as time goes on. Because you are so focused on the whole thing, what it's about, the necessity of it. The hunger strike is about the rest of your time in jail, if you are beaten on that, you are going to live your life in jail, broken, and they are going to dominate you.

I thought about dying. It didn't frighten me. Maybe you were very sad at the thought that you were going to die and all you are going to lose. You were allowed one visit a week and then, after a while, arranged special visits. Some of the other hunger strikers had a policy at the start of whenever people became ill, allowing the family in to stay with them. I think two members of the family could be there at any one time but it was only really the last three days.

Well, my father was totally opposed to it. My father hadn't visited me in jail. That was the first I had seen of him when I was on hunger strike, coming into jail. It was a combination of not sharing those political beliefs but I think just the whole thing of dealing with me in prison. He couldn't come to terms with me being in jail. 'Your mother is heartbroken.' It was a mixture of sadness and anger. 'Would you not think about this again?' I can't remember his exact words, but it was that he didn't agree with me, whereas my mother, who was the only other person I had spoken to, accepted the fact that I was on it.

Well, your sight ended up really, really bad but you still wouldn't have lost it completely. But it gets to the stage where to have the eyes open you would start to get sick because they are either twitching or you are seeing double. A lot of times when you were talking to people you kept your eyes closed anyway. People on hunger strike didn't keep drinking fluids, drinking water and salt was the only thing they took. If you stopped taking it your kidneys couldn't cope with it, so there were a lot of toxins getting into you.

A lot of people were becoming sick, vomiting a green bile liquid that would come up but it would wreck people, being constantly sick all the time, and their families watching them. I didn't have that sickness up until the very last three or four days. I suppose I watched my whole self and modelled it on other people like Tom McElwee who had been the same size as me and about the same weight when he had gone on the hunger strike. On the morning Tom died I had spoke over to him. He was sitting up in bed smoking a cigarette and about five minutes after that he just died. It must have been a massive coronary so I thought, this is the way I'm going to end up going here.

You could see the impact it was having on people. My family got in on the Friday and I remember talking to them that Friday night. And on the Saturday morning I was talking to them but I don't recollect it. And Sunday morning apparently they asked me questions. I was talking to myself or people were talking to me and I was answering. By that stage you are just totally fatigued.

I must have been slipping into a deeper level of something. Obviously, my parents had come in, my brother was back from England and they were all asking me if I wanted to change my mind. It was my mother, who had been the closest to me, who said, 'Look, if it ends up the decision is mine then I'd like to save you.' It appeared that I had lost consciousness round about dinner time on the Sunday, and my mother authorised intervention, medical intervention.

What they do in hospital is get big massive syringes and fill them with vitamins. I was rushed out to intensive care in the Royal. I came round in the Royal, and after that, it's history. You very rapidly can take foods. When I came round I was on a drip for three days and they give you all the food blended, as your stomach is small you get full very quickly. After a period I was moved down to Musgrave [Park Hospital] to the military wing so you very quickly eat all sorts of foods after it.

I don't know whether it's because your system is being bombarded with foods after such a long time that you just really perspired. You would wake up in the middle of the night just totally soaking. I was moved back to the Blocks within three weeks and normally it had been about six to seven weeks. But again I think they were trying to really pressurise the ones in the Blocks by bringing back ex-hunger strikers because the hunger strike was still going on. Nobody else died after I came off it.

By the time I went back to the Block I could still hardly see and was leaning on to the wall to get support from it. My eyes, well they still are very, very slow. That affected the whole balance system. I couldn't stop anytime. I would just get nauseous.

What I learned afterwards was that yoga helped restore the balance, which is something you could do very easily, very fluid movements. It was a slow build up to just even doing normal things like going out and walking. Now if I hadn't slept for a long time or I'd been up late studying or whatever else, I can see the same effect, the eyes becoming twitchier. I'd be walking along and suddenly take a photograph, and they'd twitch.

I can understand the situation my mother was in at that time. The whole pressure was on the families. The pressure had moved from the British Government to the families and the whole thought was that no mother could sit there and possibly watch her son die without intervening. Which is what led to the whole position to end the hunger strike, not because volunteers had stopped; there were still people lining up to join the hunger strike after the ten people had died. But it comes to a point where you say, well, it's not achieving anything.

Inside I think I have experienced a type of life – experienced emotions that are deepest. I see life ever afterwards as being an anticlimax because I feel myself that I have lived it to its full, in the sense of being on the edge of the deepest of emotions that you could experience – which are from very negative ones of anger and rage and hate to ones of exhilaration and love and comradeship. You just wouldn't have that sort of degree of comradeship or friendship to the same extent outside. So, I don't look back on it in a negative sense at all.

If I had to live it all over again I would do exactly the same. I think what happened later only happened because of the impact of the ten deaths.

6   In the Minority

William Temple was interviewed in Derry Londonderry in March 1997. He is a local Protestant businessman who has had his property damaged throughout the Troubles. He also tells of his experiences during the Troubles, including his son's imprisonment and the impact these experiences have had on his family life. William edited the transcript of his interview, so it is his story, but not entirely as he spoke it.

I have a chemist shop in Abercorn Road, a location greatly affected by the Troubles, from the first civil rights march on the 5th October 1968 to the present. Living above the shop in 1968–69, I witnessed a lot of the early rioting. The unrest intensified after the January 1969 march from Belfast, reaching a near civil war proportion after the August Apprentice Boys march, which brought in the British Army. During this period my business property was not damaged in any way, nor my turnover reduced. This was not surprising, as my shop was the last property of the Unionist majority North Ward and opposite was the only Protestant enclave in the Nationalist majority South Ward.

The Protestant enclave was small, totalling 1,400 Protestants surrounded by 25,000 Catholics. This solid block of Catholics would only have been 200 metres from my shop and linked via Upper Bennett Street, which left the property exposed to this quarter. One night during July, Nationalists broke into the Derry Jail, which was then used by the Civil Defence. The jail was in Bishop Street, and the jail wall continued down most of Upper Bennett Street, so you can imagine my vulnerability. During the rioting, a lorry was hijacked and faced towards the shop. At this stage, 2 a.m. in the morning, I left with my family and took refuge in my parents' house in Corporation Street. The next day, I bought a house in the Fountain for £350. It was in a bad state of repair and small, but as houses and flats were in short supply, I had little option. Repairs ran into September, and one morning, before I took residence in Albert Place, I turned on the radio and heard that a resident from the Fountain had been kicked to death.

6. William Temple pictured at his work in 1996. Photograph: Marie Smyth

William King was the first fatality of the Troubles in Londonderry and resulted in the Fountain being barricaded by the residents. William King was killed because he was a Protestant, so this death had an immense impact. Protestants from all over Ireland attended his funeral and it must be said, many Roman Catholics were opposed to sectarianism. It was the largest funeral I ever saw, so much was the shock and revulsion felt. Today such events are commonplace, attracting several hundreds in the cortege.

I wasn't physically or mentally forced out. It was more a foreboding that the family could be harmed. Out of thousands, four or five bigots is all that is needed to cause immeasurable suffering.

Violence did erupt catastrophically, at the outset of internment in 1971. This was the beginning of the Protestant exodus from the west bank of the Foyle. I remember helping to move thirteen Protestant families from the Dark Lane area and relocate them in empty prefabs in the Northland Estate. A large number of men with one lorry came down from the Fountain and, after negotiations with two priests from the Long Tower Parish, removed the families lock, stock and barrel between the hours of 7 p.m. and 4 a.m. The priests remained on the ground during the entire operation. These families were later re-housed in the Waterside.

I was on rota duty during the night of Bloody Sunday and vividly remember the grief and sorrow. It was not a pleasant duty and one which I felt [was] disconcerting. At dinner-time, Sunday, I was requested to prepare an antibiotic for a child. It was amoxycillin. Strange how an unusual event can fix detail in your mind. On arriving at the shop, I noticed the army had set up a gun position on the flat roof of the premises opposite the shop. As I returned home, I remember thinking this was 'over the top'.

I wasn't aware of anything untoward until I was about to open the shop at 6 p.m. A neighbour three doors from the shop asked me if I heard about the shootings and when I replied, 'No!', she said she heard there were two people shot dead during the march. As the night went on, I received more detail of the events, as many of those in for prescriptions had been at the march and were in for treatment resulting from the aftermath. It was a busy rota and it was very unsettling. The next Monday and Tuesday saw a close down of commerce and industry.

A lot of the anger was directed at Protestants, who swiftly moved to the new estates of Lincoln Court and New Buildings which were at occupation stage. Sperrin Park and Tullyally were later to accommodate many more Protestants fearful of isolation. Only one and a half thousand Protestants remain on the west bank, half in the Fountain and the rest in rural farms or mixed rural estates. Protestants had a fear of harassment and damage to personal property. It was a period of peaceful discrimination, a sort of Cold War, soon to be overtaken by damage to cars and houses during the night. Shortly after Bloody Sunday, many Protestants were bombed on the west bank, forcing many more to consider a move to the Waterside or beyond.

The Fountain, an enclave of ten cul-de-sacs bounded by the city walls, jail and commercial centre, was the only Protestant community to survive the exodus to the west side. The commercial centre became an all through barricaded area until 1985. The residents' barricades at Wapping Lane, Hawkin Street and Fountain Street were replaced with security gates manned by the army. At Fountain Street, where it faced the Long Tower, it was permanently sealed by a wall of corrugated iron and a sand centre. We would have been isolated, and cut off. Although hemmed in, we were content. We felt our houses were safe and also there was no hostile area between us and the large Protestant community on the other side of Craigavon Bridge, allowing free passage to and fro, as most of the institutions patronised by Protestants were on our side.

The demographic change was establishing a Catholic west bank and a Protestant east bank, causing a strain on cross-community relations. Mixed residential areas, particularly working class, were being phased out and so destroying the art of – not only co-existence – but also accommodation, with the need to respect and care.

I felt safe in the Fountain, which as I said earlier, was in a security sector. The Fountain population was well balanced age-wise and the adjacent periphery was mixed in 1972, although this had changed by 1976, leaving myself and five other Protestant occupants in Abercorn Road. The west bank Protestant population up to 1986 was 8,000 with over 1,000 in the Fountain. The original population in 1969 was 18,000. The removal of the security gates, after the signing of the Anglo–Irish Agreement, resulted in another mass exodus to the Waterside.

I had built up a business and my grandparents and parents had lived in the Foyle Road and Fountain from the 1880s, so I was not for moving unless I was burnt out or shot. Oh, there were days that were terrifying. Riots, shooting at security forces at the bottom of the street, and six bombs in adjacent businesses. A soldier was shot outside the shop, the bullet went through him and lodged in my shop wall. Ronnie Bond was shot dead at the house opposite my shop, and I was robbed by armed men purporting to be from the IRA.

I remember two riots in particular. I was on the telephone to Dr Spence and suddenly, there was a roar. Looking out the window, I noticed a large crowd at the top of Upper Bennett Street. I dropped the phone without replacing it and, with the staff, was out of the shop and had it locked before the crowd arrived at the bottom of the street. Then, another Thursday, Dr Hart, who had a practice at the bottom of the Abercorn Road, phoned to inform me that his premises had just been hit by gunfire and to vacate the shop immediately for my own safety. The gun battle between the IRA and army lasted ten minutes and I took the rest of the day off. The staff went down to Foyle Road and underneath the bridge to the Waterside and I went to friends in the Bogside until it was safe to go home.

To repair damage caused by vandals it cost between £300 and £1,200 per annum. Two years ago, I spent £65,000 on refurbishment, but still the defacing of the property continues. You know you are losing money, but it is accepted as a war situation, so it becomes a matter of keeping the show on the road to save your own self-respect. My commercial property is continuously damaged by sectarian louts. Weekly, they damage the stone and wooden surrounds at the front of the shop by sticks, bricks. And this week, one was using a golf club to damage the plaster below one of the windows. The night the new door went on, it was scored with Stanley knives or screwdrivers. Three external spouting systems were removed within four weeks. Eggs and stones are thrown regularly at the shop sign and windows. The door and walls are covered in slogans. I know this is the work of a gang, no more than twenty in number, and it does cause me annoyance. But balancing them are thousands of decent Catholics, and their support more than makes up [for] the financial loss.

The most I paid for one night's damage was £900. Last October I paid £200 for one night's damage, so, annually for the past odd twenty years, [I've lost] between £400 and £1,500. This, like shoplifting, reduces the net profit. [I received no compensation.] None at all. It all has to come out of your profits. It is like shoplifting, it comes out of your profits.

My children were being attacked constantly on their way to and from school. When they became older, the attacks were more vicious. I have two sons and one of them was hospitalised twice through beatings and the other, once. The eldest boy, he was in hospital twice. And after two relations were shot by the IRA, he became mixed up with the UDA. The Troubles certainly put me through the mill.

Another relation went to visit my parents in Corporation Street one Friday night and was only in the house fifteen minutes, when two gunmen entered the house looking for him. He was ordered out to the back yard and, as he moved, my mother jumped on the gunman's back, enabling my relation to escape into the street. As he pulled the living [room] door closed, the gunman shot, and the splinters of wood from the door lodged in his hair. My mother also made the street, leaving my father with the gunmen, but they didn't harm him.

She lost her voice for a fortnight and her minister obtained an emergency house in the Fountain for both of them. However, the next day, Saturday, around 2 p.m., two men called to convey their sympathy at the shooting dead of my father by the IRA. When I informed them my father was alive, they indicated a mistake had been made. They told me they had a prisoner and were sent over to inquire if I wanted to shoot him or have him shot by someone else. On finding out that the prisoner was in Irish Street Estate, I immediately made my way over. At this period, Irish Street Estate was barricaded off as a no-go area by the UDA. Declaring who I was and the nature of my mission, I was taken to the welfare clinic, which had been converted into their HQ. I informed them that my father was alive and I wanted the prisoner released unharmed. The prisoner, after others interceded, was let free without harm. Within yourself is a panic situation and your only concern is the safety of the prisoner. Personal safety is not a consideration, as the only thought is to prevent a killing. I was relieved to know he was still alive when I left.

I never had any great regard for paramilitaries. I was sceptical about their judgements and also feared the methods used to discipline their volunteers. I never told anyone until recently at a Peace Conference. Paddy Doherty was relating how Glen Barr had brought about his release at Irish Street during the no-go period. I mentioned to Paddy later, that he was a prisoner on account of a misunderstanding regarding my father.

The police discretion at this time would have been in doubt. The Protestant people felt the police had let them down and the paramilitaries were best able to protect Protestant interest. As well as that, the police had been giving Protestants a lot of hassle to enforce a ban on parades. Internment was not an issue with Protestants. The main bone of contention was the lack of police protection for Protestants who were going about their normal pursuits, and then [they were] arresting those who were forced to defend themselves, for using or having offensive weapons.

I received a phone call from [my son's] work telling me he was in hospital. The work had sent him to the bank and on the way down Shipquay Street, he was ambushed and given a severe kicking. That was about three o'clock in the broad daylight. He had a broken nose and lacerations to the face and body. The other time he received a kicking, he was almost opposite my shop in Abercorn Road. My other son was attacked in Artillery Street and was taken to hospital unconscious. One gang was apprehended and given a suspended sentence and as one of them re-offended, he was put away for three months. The main fear was that [my sons] would be attacked and after that, the fear that they would become politically involved, which usually directed them to the paramilitaries. This happened to my oldest boy.

I was surprised and shocked when the police came to raid my house at 6.30 a.m. On the Troubles, I like to keep an open mind, but I realised the eldest boy had strong opinions on politics, which at times I disagreed with. It never occurred to me that it may be some other member of the family was targeted except myself. I was involved in community work and peace negotiations, so it was possible they could have picked my name up during a raid. It was when they arrested and handcuffed my son, I realised something was wrong.

They took him in a car and gave no indication where they were taking him. I was more bewildered and I was convinced he was not involved in anything serious. He would soon be home and so, I had no feeling of hopelessness, initially. However, towards 11 a.m. the phone rang and the parent of another lad lifted advised me to engage a solicitor, as they were in Castlereagh [Interrogation Centre]. Seven were lifted from the Fountain and three from the Waterside. It was a *prima facie* case and he was on remand for two years.

I went up to Crumlin [Road Jail in Belfast] three Saturdays every month. The first visit is the worst. Nothing outside jail bears a resemblance to the inside sequence of procedure to the visiting area. It was humiliating, prolonged and unedifying. However, like everything else, you can become accustomed to it and it is then more of a social outing. No doubt, it made me aware that there was injustice. During my visits to Crumlin jail, my son pointed out other prisoners in the visiting area sentenced to life and alleged they were innocent, but had cracked in Castlereagh, admitting to anything proposed. Also, the charging of young persons from the Fountain for stealing, when they only plucked flowers from the civic flowerbed at Craigavon Bridge, left doubts about justice. My son's outlook depended on what mood he was in. Each visit was unpredictable, at times a strained relationship. In prison there is time to reflect on right and wrong, and after he witnessed a few brutal attacks in the exercise yard, a revulsion to this sort of activity set in. I am grateful he became aware of the horror of bodily harm.

The trial lasted three months and it became obvious the investigation was grossly muddled, resulting in an acquittal of [my son on] the serious charge that had kept him on remand. Four days after the trial, he was freed. I believe 'the just shall be heard' and have always approached an issue from a moral stance rather than becoming emotive. However, I did feel anger that the trial was delayed for two years. And then, to realise there was no evidence to substantiate conspiracy to murder. Minor charges were proved to prevent claims. One lad from the Fountain was found guilty of having a whistle, as part of a neighbourhood patrol and bound over to keep the peace for two years. My son came out with a couple of pounds and no further assistance.

Outside jail, he couldn't adjust. It took about nine months to get him a kind of settled. It was very difficult and then, he was nervous as well, so it wasn't an easy passage.

[We got no help.] None at all, only his church minister, the immediate neighbours – church and family. It was stressful, but at the moment, I am on no medication. I haven't had to go to the doctor at any time. Business is therapeutic and I, personally, had done nothing wrong, although I know the meaning of a broken heart. This experience and other happenings relating to the Troubles conditioned, within my mind-set, an ambivalence to life. That is how survival is possible.

After all, my wife has witnessed five violent deaths on the streets, all of them single acts. Between the court attendance and street violence, she never wants [i.e. is without] a headache. She developed stomach ulcers and became very nervous. Most days she needs painkillers and there is a tendency to find excuses not to go to social functions.

The Greysteel massacre and the Shankill bombing were close and ugly incidents, sending revulsion throughout the entire community against the gruesome evil of slaughtering unsuspecting civilians. Both communities were shocked and were motivated towards a peace settlement. The Fountain would have been a vulnerable enclave and would have heightened security for a few weeks. The residents of the Fountain have been incidental to the security policy of the day. Consideration of the security of the [average] Fountain person was not high in the Security Chief's agenda, but when the Fountain area was strategically important to the security of commerce or security establishments, the extensive security provisions benefited the residents.

During such a period, from the early 1970s to 1986, there existed a security zone and the Fountain stabilised. After security was relaxed in 1986, the Fountain population halved due to Republican attacks. No security concern for ordinary people allowed this to happen continuously. In the 1970s and 1980s we dwelt in a security zone, which meant body searches every time we went home. First it was the army, then later, civilian searches. It was like dwelling in an army barracks.

There was great relief and a sense of freedom with the cease-fires, although it must be said there was also apprehension in the Protestant community, who saw it as an IRA 'breather'. Cross-community interaction was showing signs of a comeback, but not near as extensive as pre-Troubles. The friendships and trust of the older Catholics and Protestants of the city invariably held, so the cease-fire enabled former acquaintances to be renewed, as folk felt free to move around. Cross-community activities relating to the performing or creative arts, sports and trade, never ceased during the armed conflict, but attracted more interest during the peace.

Last year saw tension and violence return to the streets. It was short but violent and, fortunately, the city pulled back from the brink. July was the worst month in the city, but coming August we fortunately, calmed down. The street violence also caused a further population shift. Protestants have again moved to the Waterside from the cityside and Catholics from the Waterside have moved to Limavady or Catholic estates in the city.

The denial of a Protestant Unionist culture goes further back than last year. Public expressions of Loyalist culture usually attract counter-demonstrations, hoping the numbers game will eventually drive it underground. The District Council name was changed, without considering the hurt to Unionists and the majority [Nationalists] decide who the minority's [Unionist's] Mayor will be, or relegate the minority Mayor should they cease to please the majority community. The style of civic leadership can change, as it now has a majority control representing the majority. Unionists' control was different, in that it was minority control, ever mindful of its limitations. Minority power is never confident, nor can it be absolute in practice. Minority rights post-1968 are now best protected by fair and honest media coverage.

Parades are part of my culture, but [do] not [make up] my [entire] culture. My concern with the parades issue and ensuing unrest is that it appears to be a war of tribal attrition replacing the armed struggle. I cannot accept that an Orange Lodge, because it is based in a village or town where its members are a minority, needs permission to be sought from the majority to parade from its hall to a local church. I strongly believe that weekday celebrations by Loyalists should not be held in majority Nationalist quarters, given the apparent threat to the other community and inconvenience. Interference with church parades usually attracts those from outside the local membership of the Loyalist Orders, and this is not helpful. It would be better if the security chiefs, or some government parliamentary agency, would restrict the number of bands and parade format in controversial areas. This would do away with any counter-protests. Anyone interfering with members of a congregation inside church, or on their way to church, must be condemned. Right to freedom of worship is fundamental to civilisation and must be protected.

The media has a duty to perform by exposure, but not the right to crescendo tension between conflicting parties. Pre-controversial parades, the media seems to have an interest in directing a spectacular outcome. The media tend to provide a platform for the extremists and bring to the fore the worst behaviour within the community. The less talk [there is] about an event, means [the] more likely [chance it has of] proceeding. During the year, little has changed to promote understanding at the coal-face but, hopefully, the desire for peace will force emotive responses to the side, to enable a calculated outcome in favour of good order. Local peace movements and business groups are seeking a genuine peace and working well within the community. I am hopeful, but media emotion and self-interest are unknown quantities.

Normality is showing signs of recovery, but a lot of patience and dialogue is still needed. It will be two steps forward and one step back. Most politicians are responsible and act with integrity. However, the ability of some could be questioned. I can see a bright future, once peace is confirmed.

I still live in the Fountain. I still have my shop in Abercorn Road, but it is up for sale now. I am getting a pension in a couple of months' time. Time to relax. The Troubles brought me into the Fountain. I most probably would have moved eventually to the leafy suburbs. However, fate placed me in an inner city, and I am now its creation. Most people can work in an inner city but couldn't live in it. The right to freedom of choice is going to become stronger and this will translate [in]to integrated housing and education.

The city appears to be recovering economically, although I stress 'appears'. Waterside Protestants still shop in Limavady and Coleraine, transferring cash from the city. Total trust among the under thirties [age-group] is still a long way off, but I believe it will come gradually.

In this city, Protestants and Unionists will always be a minority. Chinese and Indians will always be a minority. These are the facts which should not prevent any individual from full basic human rights.

7 Loss of a Father

David Clements was interviewed in June 1997 in Belfast. He is a Methodist minister in South Belfast. His father, who was a policeman, was killed on duty in 1985. As a result of his own experiences and his ministry he has become involved with WAVE, a support group for victims of the Troubles.

My father came from the Shankill Road and my mother from Ballygawley in Tyrone. They went to South Africa when they got married. I was born in South Africa. We came home for a holiday in 1969 before the Troubles started, and then came home to stay in 1970.

And as a child I was aware that something was going on in Belfast and Northern Ireland, but really I had little idea. The first impact that I can remember was at primary school. It would have been 1971/1972, when Loyalist groups were parading and marching, and paramilitaries were marching up and down the Shankill. I can remember the boys in school organising marches in play time, and we marched around the playground. I can remember thinking this was ridiculous. I would much rather have played football, but it was just an illustration of how everybody – even the children – were sucked in, even in a rural area.

Another significant event was a bomb in Dungannon. One of the boys who was in our school – I wouldn't have known him really well, he was a few years younger – but he was caught up in the bomb and was badly injured. He was critically ill for quite some time and I remember in school, the headmaster announcing this and there were prayers in the school for him. But it impacted on me somewhat at the time.

I met him subsequently, and he had taken an interest in photography. He produced a very moving, powerful exhibition a number of years ago, in which he had distorted pictures of himself. It was a very powerful thing. His face was disfigured. He had a lot of scars and he had to have a lot of plastic surgery because his face was almost blown off.

I was never really close to a bomb. My father worked in Belfast at that time. There used to be these flashes on television, 'Would key holders please return to their premises', and quite often when that happened, my father would go. I can remember some sense of worry at that time. I guess perhaps that my mother would have been more aware of the dangers and maybe it was some of her anxiety that I felt.

My father joined the RUC Reserve part-time in the middle of the 1970s. He later joined full-time. I can remember in my last year in school, my father was away for a conference, so I had the car for a few days and I took the car to school. I can remember giving a friend a lift and before I got in the car I looked underneath the car because that was my father's normal routine. I don't ever remember him telling me to do that. I don't know what I was looking for. I can remember this guy being shocked at this. To me, it seemed a normal thing to do. I can remember at times turning the ignition on in the car and wondering, 'Am I going to blow up?' I don't know that my heart rate was particularly elevated with anxiety, but I remember that was a thought that certainly did pass through my head sometimes.

There was a full-time Reserve Officer who was ambushed outside his house quite near to us. I can remember going to visit him. I would have been a medical student then. And I can remember visiting him in the hospital and talking to him on a number of occasions. He was in hospital for months and eventually he died of his injuries. That would have brought it home to me.

Another good friend of my mum and dad, who was also in the police, was attacked on Balmoral Avenue. He and his partner were shot and he was badly injured. He was in hospital for quite some time, but he survived.

Another significant thing that impacted upon me was the murder of a good friend of mine. He was a Christian and we used to meet every Friday. This particular evening I was looking forward to the continuation of a theological debate suspended at midnight the previous week. I looked around for him but he wasn't there. Towards the end of the meeting, the guy who would have been the leader of the group, he came in and told us what had happened. John was a solicitor doing his year's probation with a firm of solicitors in Belfast and he had gone to issue a summons to Andersonstown police station. As he was coming out on his motorbike, the IRA had mistaken him for someone else and they murdered him. They used an automatic machine-gun and something like fifty-seven bullets were shot into him. I think that

7. Rev Dr David Clements pictured with his daughter Ruth in their home in Belfast. Family photograph

was one of the first times I can remember feeling really shocked at something. We broke into a couple of groups and prayed. I can remember folk praying and crying at the same time.

I remember his funeral very vividly as well. I can remember singing the hymns and it was quite triumphant. There was a mix of sadness, but I don't remember a great deal of anger, although there must have been some of that, I am sure. There was also a sense of triumph, that for the Christian, death is not the end. Whatever the gangsters would do, they didn't have the final say.

The murder of my father was an evil event. It was the beginning of December and there was a Christmas party for the Youth Fellowship and we had gone for a meal. We were just leaving when someone had said there had been a phone call for me, but they had been told I had gone. Someone was giving me a lift back to my house and when we got back, there were lights on. I knew the guys I shared with were away, so it puzzled me why the lights were on and the door was open. But one of my best friends, who had lived in the house previously, obviously still had a key. So he had gone in and he was sitting there with a chap, who was the minister in the church at that particular time. I had this strange feeling. I don't know whether it was the fact that I knew there was a phone call, but I had this sense of something was wrong. When I went into the house, I saw them sitting there and I knew.

I can remember it quite vividly. It is probably not the best way to break news to somebody, but Roger looked at me as I stood in the doorway and said, 'Dave, your father has been shot.' And I said, 'Dead?' And he said, 'Yes.' I sat down on the chair and I think there was just silence for a while. Then I went upstairs to get a few things. I phoned a friend of mine, a chap that would have been in his sixties then. I don't know why he came to my mind first, but I phoned him to ask him to pray for me and I wept on the phone. I just told him my father had been killed and then I hung up.

Then we got in the car and drove to Ballygawley. This must have been about 10 or 11 p.m. by now. My father had been killed at 7 p.m. So I was really the last one of the family to get there. I can remember meeting my mother at the door. I think that was probably the most moving thing. I think the effect that it had on her was in a way the most painful thing for me.

At that time they had been attacking RUC stations. It was coming up to about seven o'clock and my father was going home for his tea. He had just left the barracks and he had gone out to his car and there was a ring at the gate. My father had said he would answer it because he was out near the gate. He opened the gate, and one or two of them had heavy calibre weapons and started firing at the station from outside. He had presumably been hit in the head by a bullet from across the road and fell down, and then he was shot again in the head at close range. Another officer was also in the yard and he was shot too. Then they carried in a bomb in a beer keg and put it at the front door, while they kept firing from outside, apparently. They then presumably drove off and one of them looked out the front and saw the beer keg and shouted to the other men in the station, who then ran out the back door when the bomb exploded. The two who died had both been shot and then the bomb destroyed the place. The other ones were quite fortunate. I don't think they were even injured apart from the odd scratch.

I remember weeping bitterly when my dad's body was brought home and it was in the coffin. We left the coffin open and I can still remember his face and the mark where the bullet had gone through his eye.

I can remember my younger sister, she would have been eleven or twelve, and she was raging at the cameramen at the funeral. There was this cameraman standing on the gatepost and she wanted to push him off. We didn't have cameras inside the church. They probably were in the church grounds and they were certainly outside our house. I was more than willing to do an interview as it was an opportunity to say some of the things that we wanted to say. There were journalists looking for interviews afterwards and my mother did some of them. It has been painful for her in many ways, but as an individual she has been remarkably strong.

At the time of my father's death my mother found – I think the whole family found – remarkable strength at that time. There must have been roughly about five hundred people who came to our house in the period of that week. I think my mother spoke a word of encouragement or blessing from the Lord to virtually every one of those people, everyone from the local parish priest to Ian Paisley. And when I look back on that time, there is a lot of pain and sorrow there, but there is also a blessing and a triumph.

I sometimes fantasised about that night. I used to think, 'What would I have done if I had been there?' (I sometimes had the car – and would have waited outside the station to pick Dad up.) In my fantasy, what I sometimes saw myself doing, was starting up the car and driving over the guy with the gun, or driving at him. Presumably, he would have been able to jump out of the way, or he may well have shot at me. Or there were other times when I thought my father's gun would have been in the house, so if somebody came and attacked the house and my father was out or something, what would I have done? I had held the gun in my hand. I probably could have used it, but if I'd had the chance and I'd had the gun, I would have shot them.

I remember my mother being worried about money and her saying to my sister, 'I don't think there'll be any more piano lessons.' That was one of her fears in those first few days, that the breadwinner was lost. In a strange way, it is helpful and in another way it has caused some hurt in a way, that financially she is secure. She has more than enough. In the preceding few years, a lot of work had been done lobbying to improve compensation and it was a lot better than it had been in the early years of the Troubles.

[My parents] never had lots of money. They had always had enough, but some of the things that they would have liked to have done, they couldn't have afforded. And now when she could afford to do them she was on her own. That was difficult.

Maybe not immediately at the time, but in the weeks and months afterwards, I did some thinking about my attitude towards them, and I did two things. My mother and I gave an interview to UTV. I can't remember now exactly what it was we said. I don't think we talked about forgiveness, but it was to say that we weren't bitter. My mother was very keen, and in a sense still is, to bring some glory to God out of all of it. She talked about my dad's faith. Even years later, I came across people who came up to me and spoke to me and said they'd seen me and my mother on television and they said it helped them.

I prayed for the people who had murdered my father and I think in all sincerity that I prayed two things. I prayed that they would be converted, and that they would leave the IRA or whatever. And if they had been converted I was offering them forgiveness. Forgiveness involves confession and acknowledgement of guilt. I can't be forgiven for my sins until I acknowledge my sins and confess them, and accept responsibility for them. I suppose the irony of it is that a lot of terrorist crime has been seen as justifiable in some way.

The other thing I prayed was, if their hearts were hardened to the point they would not change, I prayed that God would stop them doing what they had done to our family, by whatever means, and that God would bring a judgement on them swiftly. I think God answered that prayer.

When my father was murdered, they took his gun. That really upset my mother. It was the thought that somebody would be murdered with my father's gun. This would be about a year – maybe more – later and I can remember exactly where I was, to within ten yards on the road. I heard the news on the car radio that a number of terrorists had been killed in Loughgall. And just as I heard that on the radio I had this feeling in my stomach, that the people that had murdered my father were now dead themselves.

I subsequently then learned that my father's gun had been recovered at Loughgall. I know it had been used in Cookstown, although I had never inquired as to whether people had been actually killed with it. I suppose in a way I don't want to know. But I can remember that quite vividly. I don't remember ever praying for them again after that. There is no absolute guarantee that the person who callously put his gun to my father's head when he lay on the ground and finished him off, is dead. I feel that he is. It is as if that chapter is closed.

I don't think I had any anger towards God and I don't think I ever have had. I suppose there had been times when I had been angry. Perhaps it has come out at other times, subsequently, when other people have been murdered.

I remember quite a few months later, it was my aunt's ruby wedding anniversary and everyone was there. At that stage my mother's two sisters and her brother had their partners, and my mother was the odd one out because she was the only one without her husband. I remember that being one of the few occasions where I felt an anger, if not a rage, at what had happened. They had deprived my mother of her partner.

Another painful thing that remains to this day is the thought that my three daughters are missing out on having a wonderful grandad. When they were babies I took each in turn to my father's grave – the memory of those visits is still very poignant.

I am sure we must have changed in ways. It has in a sense probably led me into things that I would not otherwise have got involved in, or that I probably would not have done otherwise. I have had a pastoral concern for people who have been affected by murders and I have been able to do it in a way that I am sure I would not have been able to do without those experiences.

I have spent five years working in Woodvale. I was there when the Shankill bomb exploded. We were out shopping and I came home and I got a phone call to say that there had been a bomb. By the time I got there, it was half an hour or more after the bomb had gone off. I was digging in the rubble with the rest for a while. Two bodies were taken out while I was there. The situation was chaotic. We weren't sure what was going on, but I was with the lady whose husband owned the fish shop and her son-in-law. I took Alan and Elsie up to the Mater Hospital and I sat with them, and I was with them when they were told the worst news.

I can remember sitting in the coffee lounge on the top floor of the Mater Hospital and I had known that Alan's wife was dead. And the casualty consultant had come in and told Elsie that her husband was dead. I had known that her daughter was dead as well, and Alan was sitting opposite me, and he looked straight at me and he said, 'They've told Elsie, and I'm just waiting for my turn.' A little while later, he was told formally and that was quite difficult. I cried, but the pain I felt was more for the people than for myself.

I visited all of the folk who were bereaved. In those first few days there was some anger. The anger came more from the community generally, than from the families that had been bereaved. I suppose their initial feelings were more of shock and sadness. I would sometimes have told people that my father had been murdered. I found that it helped for people to know that this man sitting here listening to them, sometimes crying with them, had been through something similar. That did seem to help them in some way, or open up a channel through which I could help them.

I then got involved with WAVE. I've been involved with them for a few years now. I think that they are a group who have done an enormous amount of good for people in those circumstances. They really are the first (and for a long time the only group) that has been set up specifically for that purpose. They began something that nobody else had really tried to do.

I think that it has helped me too in some ways. I think it has helped me to deal with some of the feelings that I have. I think in dealing with some of the people that I have in the past three or four years, I have had more anger. And sometimes I have found that difficult to deal with. Part of it is the futility.

8   His Only Child

Iris Boyd was interviewed in her home in March 1999. She lost her father in a bomb explosion in Monaghan in 1974.

My husband and I came home from England in the early 1970s with the intention of emigrating to Australia. My family have been in business and my father and mother wanted us to stay and go into business with them. So we decided not to go to Australia. Only a couple of years later, my father was injured in the bomb. He never regained consciousness. He died four days later.

We were devastated. It was just one hole in our life – my life especially. My father and I were very close. I was an only daughter – an only child – and he brought me everywhere with him. We were just so close and I was with him that day of the Troubles.

My father and I had went into town to actually go on business. And he said to me, 'Would you call and see my aunt, if she's home out of hospital?' I said, 'Yes I will.' And he said, 'I'll meet you back here at this place' – where the bomb went off, actually.

A news-flash came on the TV that there was a bomb in Dublin. Just as I was standing at the back door with my aunt, [there was] a bang. She said, 'Come in quick, Iris. That's a bomb', and I said, 'No, it's not a bomb in our town!' I just couldn't believe it. I just would never have thought of a bomb in Monaghan town.

So immediately I said, 'Where is my father?' So I ran down the town. Every window was blown out. I can still see the town. It was a drizzly day and people were standing in amazement. When I got round to where the scene was, there was smoke everywhere. I thought it was the courthouse. But it wasn't. It was just outside Patton's Bar. Daddy had gone to get his diabetic tablets in the local chemist and had just come back out again and got into the car – and bang!

The bomb went off. He had the window down and that's why he got the shrapnel in just one wee pinhead in his head. That was the only injury he had. The bomb was right opposite where he was.

When I got round I just collapsed into a woman's arms. I came round with somebody holding a bottle of brandy to my head, to help me. Then I ran round and the police stopped me and said,

'You can't go round there because there's been a lot of bombs in Dublin and there might be more here.' I saw a cousin of mine, and he said, 'Iris, I saw your father and he's away to the hospital.' He said, 'Come with me and I'll take you up to the hospital.'

When we got to the hospital gates it was chaos. There was people lying everywhere. It was awful. I was scared to look. I met people I knew and they came in with me and sat with me. Then I saw the Reverend Heron arriving and I pleaded with him to tell me the truth. While he was away to see what was happening, dad was on the way to theatre. He said to me, 'Iris, your father is not the worst. He's bad, but he's not the worst. He's queuing for theatre. He might be all right.' I was just living in hope that he would be OK. Then I thought, 'How am I ever going to tell my mother what's happening here?' They kept asking me to phone home and I couldn't, because the phone system with us wasn't great at the time. So I phoned a neighbour of ours and he brought my mother down. Mummy collapsed. She just couldn't believe the devastation. It was awful.

Then we had to wait for hours. Nobody could tell us anything. All we could see were the stretchers coming in and all these people badly injured. It was dreadful. Our town didn't expect it at all. Monaghan Hospital coped extremely well under the circumstances. Then my aunt and uncle arrived up that night about eleven o'clock. She'd been a nurse in the hospital. Then we got up to see daddy and it was awful. He was lying bandaged completely all over his head and he was unconscious. He couldn't speak.

We were down every morning. We couldn't stay at home at all. Mummy and I just had to keep out of the house. We walked the streets in Monaghan every day. We couldn't bear to be talking to anybody. People were constantly calling and we just couldn't talk to them. That went on for four days.

Daddy put his hand out that day on the Monday. We thought, 'He's going to open his eyes and he's going to come around.' But he didn't. He just put his hand out and put his hand over my hand. On the Tuesday, we thought he's getting better, so we didn't go down. Then, my cousin was visiting my dad and she phoned me and said, 'Iris, you better get down here quick, the screen is round your father!' We went straight down and they said the worst had set in. Pneumonia had set in.

He never came round. He died at quarter to twelve that night. He couldn't be brought home. And his wishes were always, if anything ever happened to him, he was to be brought home. We

8. Scene of the Monaghan bomb in 1974, in which Iris Boyd lost her father. Photograph: Sean Boylan

couldn't do that because of the post-mortem. So he had to lie in the cold mortuary.

That day will never leave me. It was a day I'll never forget. Our life has never been the same. It was trying to overcome that tragedy. If my aunt hadn't been out of hospital, I would actually have been caught in the bomb. That's how close I was. It saved my life.

It was a very big upheaval for us after losing my father, because we didn't expect to lose him like that. My mother and I were living on medication for six weeks after the bomb. Then I realised I was pregnant. I had been taking the medication while I was pregnant and didn't realise it.

There was no counselling, there was nothing. The pain and grief we went through was hard to bear. I think it was always talked about through the family, on and off, with people always calling. That would have been the only therapy we really had. There's a lot of good to be said for wakes and everything, because it helps to bring it out.

Things were never the same for mummy. She lost a good husband, a partner in the business and the man she relied on so much with responsibilities. We had to go out and introduce ourselves to daddy's solicitor and his bank manager – we didn't even know them. That's how much my father took on his own hands. Mummy didn't want to even carry on the business afterwards, but we were forced into carrying on because of our circumstances. We had to just work hard and put crops in. I drew potatoes to Monaghan chip shops and made the best of what we had. We were very lucky to have so many good friends and neighbours in the Rockcorry area that helped us through difficult times. Our trade in business trebled as time went on. Our customers stood by us too. All this meant a lot at the time.

It was just a dreadful year for us, because Billy Fox, a cousin of mine, had been shot only two months before my father. And that was an awful blow for us when we heard first. We didn't know how we were going to break that news to my father when we heard it first.

My children were a source of encouragement to me. It was a sign of new life to me. My father would have been proud of them. I was very depressed for a long, long time and I wasn't sleeping. I put it down to post-natal blues, but looking back it was possibly the whole trauma. So much had happened in that year and it all caught up with me all of a sudden. The doctor said, 'Do you realise what you've come through? You've come through a very tough time.' It did hit me hard you know. It must have been six months or so of feeling very low and very depressed.

When the Troubles were very tense around the time Bobby Sands was on hunger strike, we got a call by our neighbour to our house on Remembrance morning in November early 1970, to say our business was on fire. My mother and staff lived above the business. Fortunately the fire brigade saved the building. It was an incendiary device. There was a man was going down the village to put a wreath on his father's grave and as he was going past my mother's door he saw the smoke. He woke mummy up and saved my mother's life.

Then we sold the business sometime afterwards. We moved to Lisburn where my husband originated from. After years in Lisburn, content and happy watching the family grow up, the Troubles peeked their head with our family once again. My son Stephen was on his way home with a friend from a fun run, when soldiers were blown up in front of his eyes as he drove behind the armoured vehicle. This was a trauma for him too. He never got over the shock of what he had seen on that day.

I've never held any hatred or any backlash on anybody after all these events hit my family. But I do ask, 'Why? Why has my family been scarred by the Troubles?' Do the politicians understand how much suffering me and other families have come through?

Well, although I love Monaghan and it's still my home, I could never live back down there again because of the memories.

I always look upon myself as never being the worst off. But when I went down to Dublin to the unveiling of the Memorial in Talbot Street, and I met the other victims in Dublin and heard their stories, I realised that their stories were equally horrific.

All I can say is that I'm glad that it's come to the stage where people are being listened to and the likes of me and the others can talk about it openly.

Although we have a cease-fire, which we are grateful [for], sadly the door hasn't finally closed, when we can all live together in peace.

9   Unintended Death

Charlotte Vij was interviewed in her home in Derry Londonderry in June 1997. Charlotte is from a Hindu family of Indian origin who live in Derry Londonderry. She is actively involved in campaigning for ethnic minority rights.

Well I was aware that I was different, that my mother wore a sari and she still does. I was aware that my parents were Indian, but that I was born here. I wasn't the first coloured baby, but I was one of the first, so there was a lot of interest. I was also the first Vij to be born in Ireland, whereas some had been born in England. We didn't have the usual set-up. My uncle sent for my father and mother to come to Northern Ireland, so they came to live in 4 Simpson's Brae, with my uncle and my aunt who was Scottish.

When I was born I was given the name Charlotte. I thought it was very unusual that my father's name was Tara Chand Vij and he came from the Punjab and that Tara is so Irish. I have always thanked God that my parents came to Northern Ireland and not England.

My father could have made more money in England, but at what price? People didn't really say a lot. I was aware that sometimes in the playground I would be called names, but then my thinking was that was not bad. I thought when I would get older, if mummy and daddy went to India on holiday, that we'd go to a place where everyone was brown and I wouldn't be different. But in reality it didn't work out like that. My memory too is of the Sikhs playing hockey. Hockey is very much an Indian game and yet I played hockey at Londonderry High School.

I was very tall for my age and, well, I had a little bit of weight on me but I was a Western fed child, not the Indian skinny child. And also my mother liked us to have soft perms, whereas over there they had long hair. I was a foreigner in my mother's country. I was a tourist. I can remember my grandfather. We were supposed to go up to see him, but I didn't want to. I didn't know him and my father was trying to make me, but I wouldn't do it. I was sorry that I didn't, because three years later he was murdered.

9. Asha Chopra, cousin-in-law of Charlotte Vij, who was killed in 1974.
Family photograph

He was murdered in August 1967. These men apparently had
drink on them, and at that time they were raising funds here in
Northern Ireland for a high school. There was nothing for the girls
in Tawwan and the receipt book had his name on it and maybe
they thought he had extra money. He'd been hurt in a riding

accident and as a result there was something wrong with his eye and he walked with a stick. His body wasn't discovered until the next day. The postman found him. That was Friday night and it was raining. In those days it wasn't as quick as now to make contact between India and Belfast. You couldn't ring direct so it took until Sunday morning, and then I found the telegram. It was the day before my O Level results, and I found my mother crying, but I didn't know why. Then to hear how he was murdered, especially with my mother and father being anti-drink. It was thirty years in August 1997 since my grandfather was murdered. It seems like yesterday.

Well, I can remember that Saturday [in] October 1968. It was my last year at the Londonderry High School. I wasn't there on Duke Street, but the scenes were shown on television. On the Monday there was a lot of talk in school and we thought it was great that Bernadette Devlin, despite her West Belfast background [sic], eventually became an MP. I had lived in the Waterside and I didn't know what was going on in the Cityside. My father had a shop in Butcher Street, in the Diamond. It was only when the Troubles started that we found out what was going on.

At my primary school, one day these Protestant women asked me the question that I dreaded them asking me. They would say to me, 'How many children are in your family?' and I would say 'I am the eldest of seven.' 'Oh your poor mother, what she went through, she must have gone through terrible times!' And I thought this was a crime. Then when the Troubles started and I heard about people in the Bogside, who had twelve children and the fathers weren't working!!! How did they manage? The mothers were working in the shirt factory to keep the families and they were having to go up to the Crown Buildings to collect the men's [social security] money – they had to get the money before the men would gamble it. So I learnt all these new things.

Derry had been deprived, and industry didn't go west of the Bann. I remember our teachers went to Coleraine to protest that the new university wasn't coming to Derry. The teachers came back and said it was no good, they couldn't stop it. I remember the hurt that it had gone on for so long. People didn't have 'one man one vote', the British Government just ignored that, and the Government at Stormont also ignored it. I just thought it was dreadful. I didn't realise that people didn't have the right to vote and I didn't think that a Protestant Council controlled my city.

The children that I played with were Catholics because Protestants didn't really live nearby. They knew my mother wore a sari but we didn't talk about religion, they didn't question it. We weren't like today's children who ask each other, 'What religion are you?' We played innocently, we didn't know. I knew they weren't Protestant because they didn't go to my school but we played very happily. I didn't go into chapel because I knew I wasn't a Catholic.

I have been so lucky to live where I do, because my brothers and sisters in England suffer daily racism. I went for nine months to a college outside Liverpool, and out of over 1000+ students, I think there were ten to twelve students of the ethnic minorities, so it wasn't like it is today, with so many different races. I stayed nine months and I got depressed. I have a lower mood disorder that occurs in the winter months, something similar to SAD [Seasonal Affective Disorder]. I didn't want to teach, so I came home but my father when he collected me in Belfast he said to me, 'Why have you come home? There are no jobs here.' My first job was in the Crown Buildings, that was December 1970. So I did get a job.

While I was there Bloody Sunday happened, so all the Catholics walked out on the Monday and came back on the Thursday. Two Protestant girls walked out in sympathy with them. The rest, we all stayed and we worked. There was ill feeling for some time that they had all walked out, and I think that there were protests to Ian Paisley about it. People were shocked, stunned, that the British Army could do that.

I call the British Army the British Imperial Racist War Machine! I believe the army should leave Northern Ireland. Young soldiers got murdered. I thought it was wrong. I believe in non-violence. Mahatma Gandhi was regarded as a saint by my parents. He was the greatest man that ever walked the face of this earth, so I believe in non-violence – I can't accept violence.

I was the first born and the eldest got it hard. My parents came from a strict environment where the sexes were kept separate, marriages were arranged, and you did not mix. So we were living here and well my father tried to keep me away from men. So, at the age of twenty-one, I left and went to Belfast. I got a transfer very quickly because nobody wanted to go to Belfast and I felt I needed to live my own life. I wanted my freedom and I just had to go. I hadn't really suffered racism in Derry because my father, he was very, very well known. They knew our background, they knew where we came from. But going to Belfast and living in East Belfast where people were Protestant, I was a lone stranger. I was a lone person, I was coloured and this was 1972.

It was very difficult for me with my colouring, I stood out a mile. Short of mummifying myself, I cannot hide away. I was asked questions, because when you're a stranger people want to know your background. I was asked where I came from, so I used the full title – I said Londonderry. What part? The Waterside. What schools did you go to? Protestant. Are you a Protestant Hindu or a Catholic Hindu? Nowadays it's a joke, but it wasn't a joke then. I was surprised at the ignorance of them. There was this thing that you had to find out which side anyone who came new into an area supported. I was shocked, because in my own Waterside or in the Cityside no one ever asked me, because they knew my family.

The Troubles were very bad. I did meet up with racism. I met up with racism due to the fact Belfast was predominantly Protestant. And even though my two aunts were Protestants, there were Protestant men who maybe fancied to take you out because you were a novelty, because you were coloured. You attract a lot of attention but you were being used. Protestant men said I would never marry because I was the wrong colour for them, so that was hurtful. Time has moved on, now there are so many mixed race marriages in Northern Ireland, hundreds and hundreds.

I also was amazed at the Workers' Strike 1974. I lived in a very Protestant area and I had known before that RUC Land Rovers would be set on fire in my own city but this was a Protestant street and it was Protestants who were doing it. They threw petrol bombs and it went on and on. At the time of the Workers' Strike I was in the Civil Service and people walked to work. So that's what I was doing. Well, it was sad, but it was funny as well because I was wearing an orange coat. I had kind of a smock coat and it was checked. It was different colours but it was predominantly orange. I couldn't believe it that these men were walking along screaming 'Black Bastard' at me. There were hundreds and hundreds of them and there was one Land Rover and a few police. I often wondered what would have happened if some of them had tried to beat me up. How would the police have coped with that?

I told one or two people that that had happened and they said 'Oh how awful' and I buried that until last year. I didn't talk about it until last year. Here were these men wearing masks for a start, which was menacing, but the fact that they had screamed 'Black Bastard' – that was one of the worst times of my life.

I only stayed in Belfast five years, then I came back to Derry. I have been campaigning to get the Race Relations Act. It's become my work now outside my work. I'm on the radio a few times a year and I get local articles published. Now the Commission of Racial

Equality has been established in Belfast. I went to their first meeting and now they're coming to Derry. I go and talk to groups if they want me to.

I went in to the Oakgrove Integrated School to talk to the students and I sat on the stage and they started asking questions. One was 'Has the Troubles affected you?' I told her very briefly that my cousin's wife had been shot dead. She was shot in the head. She was going to have a baby, so that was two people murdered. I wasn't feeling very well at the time, so I didn't tell her the full story but I did tell her it was very hard.

Asha Chopra had only lived in Northern Ireland for seven years. She considered herself Indian. I didn't, because I had only seen India two months of my life, so I felt Northern Irish. But she was Indian and she wore a sari. A few days before she was murdered, an Indian man who lived a few doors from her had a terrible accident at Ballerena. A train decapitated him, and on the Friday she went to the funeral. When you go to a crematorium you think about death. So that night in bed with her husband, she said things to him like, 'If I die and you marry again, make sure your second wife is good to my children.' And he said, 'Don't be so stupid! You won't die, and I will never marry again.' The next afternoon she was murdered.

That morning, she had a bad cold and her husband said, 'Don't go out!' But she didn't listen. She drove across – literally across – the road to the supermarket, and she had her two children with her. Unknown to everybody, the IRA had set up an ambush. They took over a house and a young man of seventeen years of age pulled the trigger. He fired one shot only at the policeman who was telling her to move. She had the window rolled down. The bullet – the one bullet – severed an artery in his arm and hit her head.

A lot of people came running to help her and they took her away. But she died very quickly in hospital. My brother rang from the shop to say to my mother, 'Asha's been shot.' So she thought [that] she's been shot in the leg, and that she was going to live. She didn't realise how serious it was. So an Indian man came and took my mother and my aunt to Altnagelvin Hospital. And when my mother asked to see Asha Chopra, someone came to her and said, 'I'm sorry she's dead.'

She was only twenty-four years, and she was four months pregnant. She was completely innocent. She hardly came out of her house. She was a family woman wanting to bring up her children and not be involved in anything. The wrong place at the wrong time. I thought it was so cruel that someone could pick up a gun and murder in cold blood. I know they were aiming for someone else. I know they didn't aim for her. I was working in a school in Belfast and my brother had been trying to get through to me. I went up to my room to listen to the 1.55 p.m. news. The news told me that Asha Chopra had been shot dead. So I broke down.

The next day we went to the crematorium and Asha was cremated, and her unborn baby. The surgeon had told my father that it was better she died because she would have been a vegetable. I'd never seen a dead body and I didn't want to see Asha's body. She was in the corner and everyone said she was bandaged and they put a sari on her, but I didn't want to see her. I couldn't face it. She was like a child in the sari, she was tiny. She had beautiful brown hair. She was beautiful, and for me it was so wrong. I will never ever forget what they did!

The following Monday a woman came to start work. She had read about it and she sympathised. She was a Christian and she sympathised. People always said to me that the ones who had taken over the house, they couldn't have been Catholics. They were Catholics in name, but they couldn't have been Catholic because they wouldn't have done that. I couldn't understand and when I went back to Belfast for a while I wouldn't go into Catholic areas. I wouldn't go into Smithfield. I blamed all Catholics for that. Then I just had to say to myself, 'You just have to wise up! You can't go round like that! You have to get on with life.'

I still think about her. My family doesn't really, but I still do think of her. To this day I have a framed photograph of her and her husband. I thought of her baby and what age her baby would have been. It destroyed her family because her husband had to take the two children to India, because he wanted to sell his business and his house. Luckily my sister was out there in India, so she was able to help. He went back to India and it took him a long time to remarry, but he did. And he has another son and daughter.

Now the compensation was £3,900 because as a housewife she wasn't really insured. She didn't really get much and that was held in trust for her children when they grow up. So her children came back to Northern Ireland. The daughter didn't stay. She went back to India and she's married. The son, he came back to work in Coleraine and he married and he has a son himself. I still feel that it was very, very traumatic.

A book called the *Irish Raj* came out and I helped with the research. I used my small photograph of Asha Chopra and they enlarged the copy and it is included in the book alongside the actual incidents. Her funeral was small. Most people did not connect her with the Vij family and then eventually they found out. But what could you say to the family who were bereaved?

Well the thing was too, my brothers you see, because the business was credit, they had to go round collecting money. They were immune [from attack] and nobody was allowed to do anything to them, but then younger people growing up started to do things. My father, I can remember in October 1971, he was hit over the head with a gun. This had never happened before. It ended up that my father had to put his money into his socks. He'd come in the backdoor of our house in Rossdowney Park and there was a chair and he used to sit and take money out, and I watched that. That was a big change.

Normally you were free to go out and do your business, but these younger ones growing up had no respect. The Indians who went round collecting money were supposed to be immune from all of it because they were providing a service, so that working-class people paid up for their clothes that they couldn't afford.

I do like living here but so many people have moved. I love this country so much, yet I cannot accept the violence and I cannot accept the fact that if the Troubles cease, racism will increase. People have to find a victim for their hatred. With the attacks on the Chinese community last year, the Chinese got worried in Derry and then the Indians were saying, 'It's the Chinese now, it will [be] the Indians next!' So people got very scared. The British Government passed the Race Relations Act in England in October 1976 and it took nearly twenty-one years to become law on the 4th August 1997. It was important because discrimination was happening in jobs and if people wanted to do anything about it they had to do it on religious grounds and not on the grounds of racism. It has been recognised in law but you cannot legislate, you have to educate people. Laws are broken. It didn't work in England but then England has a greater ethnic minority.

We have a very small ethnic minority in Northern Ireland, the Chinese being the largest group. The Indians were here first and then the Chinese came in the 1960s. They had a lot of problems and also they kept within their own. They didn't tend to inter-marry. They were isolated and the locals thought they didn't want to mix. They worked unsociable hours until late and they had language difficulties.

Northern Ireland is becoming so racist. I don't want race to become an issue in Northern Ireland. That's why I fight every day. I want to educate people in racial awareness. With our Troubles, parents did not teach their children to respect other religions. How can they teach them to respect other cultures? People who are born and brought up here feel as Irish as them but have got a different colour of skin because of their parents.

They've done studies in England and they have found that children don't tend to be racist but when they are watching programmes on TV, their parents are calling people on TV derogatory names. The children then take that into the playground and this is what is happening in Northern Ireland too. When I was a child I was called a 'heathen'. That came from the parents, not the children.

I watched a programme, a BBC 2 Network East, called *The Hidden Troubles*, aptly named, 'Racism in Northern Ireland'. These questions had not been addressed because there was no law. This Chinese woman came on television and said in Northern Ireland that these rowdy men came in and she knew there would be trouble, because they had drink on them. They beat her up. They broke her ribs and they got away with a fine. The man beside her said, 'A good day for me in Belfast is a day without abuse!' I couldn't stand that and that made me write to the Chief Constable. I thought, 'No! I couldn't have this! This is my Northern Ireland!'

I'm proud of my colour, proud of my background and proud of my heritage. I cannot accept that I'm inferior to anyone in Northern Ireland. I can't accept it. I do not think I could live anywhere else. Fate decreed I be born here. I have travelled to many countries, but this is the best.

10   All in a Day's Work

William Rutherford was interviewed in Belfast in October 1997. He is a retired consultant from the Casualty Department at the Royal Victoria Hospital, Belfast. He worked in the Casualty Department throughout the worst period of the Troubles and is now involved in Corrymeela, a Christian ecumenical cross-community organisation which works for peace and reconciliation in Northern Ireland.

I was born in 1921 in Warrenpoint. My father was the Presbyterian minister. I was six when we moved to Dun Laoghaire and a new life in what was then called the Irish Free State. I have vague memories of older people at that time talking about the Troubles. I think they were referring to the old IRA and the Black and Tans. It was many years later that I became aware of the Civil War in the South. I think most Protestants in the Free State were not involved in the Civil War and did not talk much about it. Though my home was in the South, we went for holidays each year to Kilkeel, near the Mourne Mountains.

From 1934 to 1939 I was a boarder in Campbell College, Belfast. So although my home was in the South, I was still in contact with the North. Most of my relations lived there. Then in 1939 I went to Medical School in Trinity College in Dublin. I qualified as a doctor in 1944 and was appointed as a House Surgeon in the Belfast City Hospital. I was married in 1945, and in 1946 we went to Edinburgh. Then, in 1947, my wife and I went to India and I worked in a mission hospital in India from 1947 to 1966. I had four months of the British Raj. India got its independence in August 1947. We lived there for almost twenty years. Our three children were born and lived their early years there, and we were drawn deeply into the life of the local community. All those things are clues to my identity.

I suppose in our more recent Troubles from 1968, people became aware of the importance of their identity. Most Catholics felt they were Irish, most Protestants felt they were British, though some felt both British and Irish. As I thought about my own identity, I realised that I was both British and Irish and part of me was Indian also. People are not just individuals, we are persons, and we are persons in a community. We become what we are within the community. This can powerfully affect our feelings, our perceptions and our behaviour, and often we are unaware of this.

After our return from India in 1966 I obtained a post in the Casualty Department in the Royal Victoria Hospital. I felt that Belfast was my city – the whole of it. Some people never went into certain areas, feeling threatened there. Once you stopped going into a certain area, you very quickly got a phobia about the people that lived there. So I deliberately drove through both Protestant and Catholic areas. At that time, O'Neill was the Prime Minister. He was going to introduce a whole new political arrangement. There would be no second class citizens. Brian Faulkner was the Minister of Commerce and he was going to make us really prosperous, with lots of money and lots of employment. The word 'ecumenical' had been discovered and people actually knew what it meant. So 1966 to 1967 was a very exciting time.

When the Civil Rights campaign started, I wondered if the things they were saying were really true or not. I found it really difficult to find out. I never actually went to any Civil Rights demonstration. But today I feel badly that I didn't get involved. I had joined the Corrymeela Community almost immediately on my return from India. At that time it was a totally Protestant community, a Protestant community that was looking for reconciliation with Catholics. But when the rioting and the burning of houses started, our buildings in Ballycastle became a place of refuge. Some of the people who had lost everything lived there. Then we changed our rules and accepted both Protestants and Catholic members.

In 1967, the Casualty Department in the Royal was situated in antiquated quarters, and out-patient clinics of different specialities were scattered here and there all over the campus. Then they built a great new building, with all the out-patient departments on the upper floors and the casualty down on the ground floor. We moved across in April of 1969 to vastly improved facilities. This was just in time, for on the 2nd of August 1969, the Troubles in Belfast started with a bang.

In the beginning, I would be working just as normal during the day. Then in the evening somebody would give me a phone call, at about maybe eight o'clock or so. I would go back down to the hospital and I would be there [working] until 2 a.m. or so. I listened to the news and was trying to understand what was going on.

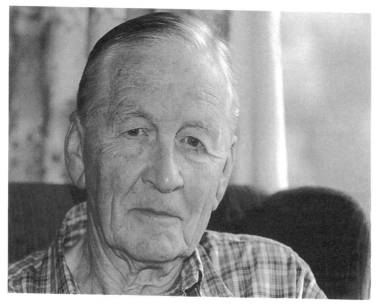

10. William Rutherford, retired consultant in the Royal Victoria Hospital, Belfast. Photograph: *Irish News*

From the 2nd until the 15th of August, there was rioting on the streets almost every night. It was largely people pulling up pavements and throwing great chunks of stone at each other. Then they started burning houses. I heard that the B Specials were there and they and the police were involved in the rioting. I didn't know what to believe. I suppose coming from a middle-class Protestant background [it] had its effect on me and my attitudes to the police. As that fortnight went on I got more and more tired. I was also labouring under the delusion that I was indispensable!

Suddenly on August 15th the troops came in. I slept in the hospital that Saturday night. On the Sunday morning everything was quiet and I went out on to the Falls Road. All the barricades blocking the side streets were down. I went home and had breakfast and came back in.

When I was finished, I went across the Falls Road and went up the side of St Paul's Church. There was a small hall a little further up. Here were these people who had been burned out of their homes the night before. There was this old man and he was sitting rocking from side to side and he was saying, 'Our young lads were wonderful, our young lads were wonderful. If it hadn't have been for our young lads I don't know what we would have done. Ah, but they had no rods, they had no rods.'

I suppose for me the Troubles were always about real people and I was meeting them. If somebody was found to be dead on arrival at hospital or if they got into the resuscitation room and then died there, it was my responsibility to break the news to the relatives. So I met Catholic families, I met Protestant families, I met paramilitary families and I met families with no political involvement. The outstanding thing, from my point of view, was the humanity of everybody, which was so much more obvious to me than the things that were supposed to be the differences.

Dealing with injuries, in order to do your work efficiently I had to think in terms of: 'What is the blood pressure?'; 'What is the pulse rate?'; 'What is the haemoglobin?'; 'Where can I get a needle into a vein to get a blood transfusion going?'; 'Do I need to take X-rays?'; 'Is there a bed?'; 'Is there an operating theatre available?' and so on. It was a technical problem, and solving it was almost like solving a crossword puzzle.

During the worst periods I would have been involved with maybe eight seriously injured people on a bad day, and at the end of it, I really hadn't made an emotional relationship with any one of them. Then they would have been moved from casualty to a surgical ward, where they might have been nursed for three weeks and might have died at the end of that time. By that time, the staff would have known the whole family. My position was a bit different. So, although I saw a lot of patients with severe injuries who went on to surgical wards, this didn't affect me emotionally the way the deaths did.

One day Gerry Adams was wheeled in with a bullet through his chest. I had often wondered if someone like Gerry or Ian Paisley were to come in what would happen to my emotions. Actually, his technical problems were fairly straightforward and I knew what to do. I did it just the way I would have done for anybody. It was only when it was all over that I looked back and wondered, 'Gracious me! That was Gerry Adams and what did I feel?' But I didn't really feel anything different while I was treating him. He was a human being, like any other in need of help, and I was glad to be doing something positive.

I was very glad of my friends in the Corrymeela Community because this gave me a place where I could go and unburden with people who allowed me to talk over what was happening. One day, I was sitting in the Corrymeela Centre and looking out to Rathlin. This was a weekend for members of the Community. There was a woman sitting – there were only the two of us, I think, in this big room. And I said to her, 'I'm sorry, I'm afraid I don't know your name.' Then she gave me her name and I remembered at once. Maybe a year before, I had had to break the news to her, when she arrived at hospital, that her husband had been shot dead. She was a Catholic and I a Presbyterian. But after this we became close friends. I always wanted to learn the truth about what was happening across divides like this, but I did not find it easy.

From the beginning, I have wanted justice and wanted peace for everybody but it took me quite a while trying to learn, trying to discover where justice was. I remember after Bloody Sunday, I was glad to hear that a learned English judge had been put in charge of the inquiry. I remember waiting and hearing his report. To me, this was just the truth. Afterwards I heard all the objections and denials. At first I thought, 'There's some people can't accept the truth!' It was a long, long time before I realised that having a learned British judge in charge is no guarantee of detachment and objectivity.

When Mrs Maguire and three of her children were killed on the Andersonstown Road, the dead and injured were brought to my department. So I got to know Mairead Corrigan and Betty Williams, the Peace Women who received the Nobel Peace Prize. I went to many of those marches. By the end of 1972, there were all these different peace movements. There was PACE and Corrymeela and Women Together and the Peace People and so on.

Then in October 1972, there was Bloody Friday, when there was a whole series of bombs in Belfast. There was a man called Reverend Joe Parker and his son Stephen was killed. He was a Church of Ireland Minister. He started his peace movement called Witness for Peace. Each year he arranged a service at the City Hall. Small metal crosses were set in the grass for all the people that had been killed in the Troubles. I thought if we all, from the many peace groups, put our shoulders together maybe we could be more effective. So, in December 1972, I put an advert in the paper suggesting that all the peace groups should cooperate. The umbrella body was to be called 'Action for Peace'.

At that point the different peace bodies were not ready for joint action. Really, if we had been called 'Inaction for Peace' it might have been more accurate. But a small group of those people continued to meet once a month over a period of fifteen or eighteen years. Most of those people would have been from Falls and Shankill. It was mainly a working-class body. It also contributed to my education. It was a very small movement, but I think it was important to the people who were in it.

In 1979 or 1980, my wife and I joined Fitzroy Presbyterian Church. Shortly afterwards the minister, Reverend Ken Newall, asked me to help in forming a group in the church to work for reconciliation between Catholics and Protestants. Out of this grew the Clonard Fitzroy Fellowship. It was open to anybody who worshipped in the Catholic Church at Clonard Monastery or Fitzroy Presbyterian Church.

In the beginning, our programme was Bible Study and things like that. Then we started looking at the contentious issues like discrimination. I wrote to Bob Cooper, the head of the Equal Opportunities Commission, and asked him to come and talk to us. Our friendship allowed us to talk frankly to each other. After his address, we broke up into small groups and we exchanged our own experiences and emotions. This was just one of many similar topics that we discussed. A few families in Fitzroy objected and left the church because we were talking with Catholics. But many new families came to join the church because it was open to such change.

In 1996, at the time of the Drumcree march, and the disturbances that followed, I had been up in Corrymeela Knocklayd for four days over the 12th of July. When I returned to Belfast there had been rioting and burning of buses in West Belfast. I wondered what on earth was happening to my friends from the Clonard Fitzroy Fellowship who lived there. I rang a couple of people, and the second woman I rang said, 'Oh I've just been longing that the Clonard Fitzroy group would meet.' So then I started ringing round inviting the Protestant and Catholic members. Then everybody came to my house and we sat around and we just told our own stories. Some of them were stories of the immediate past and some of them were memories, away back years and years earlier living in places like Short Strand. Everybody's story was heard and everybody accepted and affirmed.

So in a way I'm very privileged. My job, my church connection and my membership of the Corrymeela Community allowed me to hear the hopes, the fears, the pains and joys of both communities. In order to recover from this communal mental illness which has caused our Troubles it is essential for the top representatives of our communities, the politicians, to negotiate on our behalf. Politics are very important. Being a politician is not at all easy. So I wish them all up at Stormont the best of luck. I don't underestimate the problems that they have got.

I, myself, made little impact on politics. But I hope I have made some contribution in working from the bottom up. That is where, gradually, you can get attitudes changed and help to create a different kind of atmosphere. This then allows the politicians to do things that they wouldn't otherwise have been able to do. So I hope that I haven't been entirely useless. It has been profoundly enriching for me. I think that my political understanding has been lifted forward a great deal.

My social understanding has been lifted forward and my whole religious life has benefited enormously. There have been tears and heartaches, but there have also been joy and hope and that surely is where our future lies.

11   'That was the last time I seen him'

Paul Morrissey was interviewed in his home in Belfast in December 1997. His father was killed by a Loyalist gang who came to be known as the Shankill Butchers. After identifying his father's body, Paul was left with very distressing after-effects.

I got home from work and my mother told me my father was dead. But then, within a couple of seconds, his photo came up on the TV. I remember seeing his picture on the TV, but the TV was turned down. So, I knew he hadn't died of natural causes, like a heart attack or stroke. I knew it was something bad, or his picture wouldn't have been on the TV. So she told us what had happened; that his body had been found in Glencairn and it looked as if it was the Shankill Butchers. I was still trying to take it in when the police came to the door for us to go and identify the body.

I remember it was a whole discussion, why I should go or not because I wasn't eighteen yet. So, my older brother said, 'Well, he's got a right to go, if he wants to go.' So, we went up. I can remember it as well as if it was yesterday because it was a really bad night, really lashing with rain and we were sitting in the car and the rain was beating off the car and you could see the lights on in the entrance to this morgue.

When we got there the detectives said to us, 'We haven't finished stitching the body up, so you will have to wait a while.' But before we went in he said, 'We'd like youse just to look at the face and don't look at the body.' It struck me as, just, 'Why not?' But I would have been willing to go along with that, but my other brother, he wasn't. And he said, 'I want to see the whole body.'

I didn't even think it was my da. I thought there was a mistake. Even when they pulled the blanket off him, it was a good five minutes before I realised it was him. It was my other brother – he knew the instant they took the blanket off him that it was my da. He broke down. I didn't break down and my older brother, he is powerful like my da in a lot of ways. He's a terrible strong type of

11. Paul Morrissey pictured with his daughter Megan in their home in September 1999. Photograph: Marie Smyth

person. I could see him trying so hard to compose himself. His lips were shaking and his whole face was contorted. But me, I was just dumbfounded. I couldn't believe it. I couldn't cry. I was just trying to take in this sight that was before me, and come to terms with it. But when my brother pulled the blanket off, the two detectives stepped away back because I think they were trying to give us a bit of space to deal with what we were looking at. It was a very personal thing but it was very hard to deal with.

We stood with the body about fifteen minutes. There wasn't many words exchanged. My older brother, he was just devastated, he couldn't even talk. You couldn't put it into words. I was looking at this thing. It resembled a piece of beef that had been beat with hatchets and hammers and stabbed, and fingers missing and nose stitched back on the face, head caved in, throat cut right back to the spinal cord. I was taking all these details in. You probably go through your whole life and never see a sight like that.

I got hardly any sleep at all. There was a lot of people coming and talking about the old days, when they knew him. There wasn't much talk about the state he was in because people were trying to be delicate about it. I was able to talk away. I think I just switched on to autopilot then and tried to detach myself from what I'd seen.

I was still trying to stay aloof from it all. It was like something that was surreal. It was as if I was watching something, but I wasn't actually a part of it. I wasn't sort of grief stricken at this stage. I think I was still trying to take in what I'd seen.

Then, a couple of nights into the wake, these thoughts started entering my head. I wondered, before they killed him, 'Was he begging them to kill him?' – because he must have suffered terribly. I wondered was he saying to them, 'Put an end to it.' Maybe they took longer about the job in order to make him suffer more. I used to have them thoughts. The frustration – I could have killed somebody in the frustration. I think I was very, very close to taking revenge, very close to it.

The nightmares seemed to be based around the part where he was begging for his life. I always remember my da as a sort of well-built type of guy who was able to look after himself. I wonder – did they break him down, did he beg like a dog? Or I wonder was he a man to the end? It's all stupid now, when I look back on it. It's all immaterial now. I'm sure, had I been in that position I would have begged like a dog. Certainly I would have squealed like a pig – or if they had asked me to quack like a duck – for them to end it. But this had embedded itself in my head and it stuck there. And I couldn't seem to get over this hurdle. Did he beg for his life? I could see these figures surrounding him, beating him with hatchets and hammers, stabbing him. And then finally finishing him off by cutting his throat. I could see this helpless figure surrounded by these ones, just like a pack of hungry animals that you would see on a wildlife programme, tearing a wild beast apart, or something. That was the kind of visions I was having. I had dreams where the hair on my head was standing, the sweat would be just dripping off me. I didn't have nightmares every night, but it got worse later on.

I remember the day he got buried. I remember, I never cried until the day that we buried him. As soon as the dirt hit the top of the coffin, it was unbelievable. I think I knew it was final then. I wasn't going to see him again. That's what brought it home to me, a piece of clay hitting the top of a mahogany box.

I didn't worry so much about the crying. I've learned over the years to let go of the macho thing about crying. In fact, there's times when I sit and cry on my own, sometimes it's great just to do that, the relief is brilliant. Certain moods would bring that on. Something might happen on the TV, or somebody loses a brother or sister or father and I'd really feel for them. I know what they're about to go through.

I wondered how my kind of God could let this happen. He was a man that attended chapel every day. I don't think I even gave God a second thought then. Any grief that I was feeling was being overpowered with this feeling of hatred.

It got worse again, and I think it got worse because I had never addressed it properly in the first place, because I didn't know how to. At that time I wasn't the sort of person to say, 'I need to talk to somebody. Can you help me? There are things inside me that I need to get out. Would you sit and listen to me for a while?' I'm still not that type of person. Very rarely would I talk about it. Although the anger got less, the bitterness and the hatred started to take over and instead of actually wanting to go out and physically take revenge, I found myself wishing it on them and hoping that the paramilitaries on our side would go and plant a bomb and kill so many. I found myself going towards that mentality of it.

I left and went to England and worked over there another thirteen years. My marriage hadn't worked out and I was just beginning to hate this place anyway, and what was going on in it. I just wanted to live some sort of life with a bit of normality in it. I thought that if I ran to England I might escape. I must have been totally confused and didn't know which end of me was up or down.

I was a Jekyll and Hyde type of character and I was aware of it, but I didn't know what to do about it. I took drink, tablets, tranquillisers, and Valium. Anything I could get my hands on. Usually drink. The drink would stop it for me up until the first half a dozen pints. Then magnified it after that and all the things that you are trying to get away from just get bigger. And then, when you're drunk, the frustration seems to get braver and wants to show its face. And it comes out, and it's the people that are closest to you that suffer then because your abuse is directed at them, although they did nothing to deserve it. But that's who ends up taking the brunt of it. I would kick, punch doors, put holes in doors, beat my head off walls. I would do that, all right.

I would feel it most if there was a bomb explosion and there were a couple of soldiers or something killed. When I would go to work, and everybody at work would be saying, 'There's them Irish bastards again, another couple of young innocent lives.' I'd be saying, 'Do youse really know what it's all about?'

I felt jealous a million times, wishing I could have the life that other people had. I wished I could find it as easy to get up and do the mundane things every day that they were finding easy to do. I couldn't. I didn't know the reason why. But the reason why was that I was mentally disturbed because of what I'd seen and the effect it had on me, and the people around me. I was very close to the men in white coats taking me away, and any authority or any say I had over my own life and destiny would have been taken away from me. They would have locked me up somewhere and said, 'Hey, this guy is a danger to himself and society, we may throw that key away.' It was very real and very frightening too.

Before I left and went back to England I was taking tablets and drinking and falling down in the street and knocking myself out and people were lifting me and bringing me home. I felt I had to remove myself from it because I was bringing disgrace on my ma, because people were saying, 'You know, your son was drunk the other night and he fell and split his head open there, you know.'

When I came back from England I suffered from bad depression but I could never explain what was wrong with me, because I was scared of people thinking I was an absolute nutcase, which everybody ended up thinking anyway. It was a slow train coming. The nervous breakdown was well on its way. It was inevitable. I wasn't dealing with what was going on in my head. I was trying to cover it up either by drinking or taking tablets, trying to escape some other way.

I was out with a lot of friends one night and I really enjoyed myself, but I was suffering from severe mood swings. I'd fell out with my wife at the time and was staying with my mother. I remember coming in home, I was drunk and I could see my ma looking at me. She didn't have to say anything to me, I knew what she was saying to herself, 'He's going to destroy himself.'

There was that much stuff in my head, I couldn't say to myself, 'I'll tackle A tomorrow and I'll tackle B on Tuesday.' I couldn't gel anything, everything was just jumbled – so I cut my throat. I went to bed and smoked a cigarette and cut my throat and pulled the blankets up over me and that was it.

My mother found me. The next I knew I was in the intensive care unit in the hospital. And then from there on into Ward 10, which is the psychiatric unit. I wouldn't take any medication. They wanted to give me electric shock therapy and I wouldn't take that either because I'd seen what it was doing to other people in there and I was scared. I really started to get frightened that any responsibility I had or any say I had over my own life was going to be taken away from me. I was fighting hard to hold on to any sanity I had left.

Some of the nicest people I've ever met in my life, I met them in Ward 10. Just ordinary people like me, just trying to deal with what was going on here.

The reason I done it was because I'd considered other ways of doing it. I'd considered hanging myself. But I was always scared of falling the wrong way and maybe ending up in a wheelchair, and somebody having to wipe me, and feed me, and clean me for the rest of my life. I was scared of taking an overdose in case I just ended up damaging the kidneys that bad that I'd end up bedridden. So I knew what I was doing but I never give any consideration to what I could have done to my family and to my kids. I was just totally selfish.

My mother had a stroke shortly after it. Although nobody has ever blamed it on me, I'm sure people have thought, 'Had she not have found him.' She had to lift me out of the bed and drag me into the living room to phone the ambulance. I never thought of any of that.

The stay in the psychiatric unit definitely made me stronger. It was as if somebody had opened a door and let me look in somewhere and see that you'd better get to grips with this now. It also let me see that there were other people like me because of certain things in their lives that they couldn't handle, so I wasn't on my own. The doctors, I don't think really done me much good. You have your own psychiatric nurse, they always had plenty of time for me, and I probably spoke more to them ones than I ever did in twenty-two years.

But the doctor would walk in and he'd have a folder with your name on it and he'd say, 'Can you count from 135 backward deducting two every time?' And you would do it and he would say, 'What day is it today? What month is it? What date was it last Thursday?' The conversation would last ten minutes and he'd shake your hand and say, 'Well, I'll see you next week.' If that is personal treatment, they can shove it. That wasn't the kind of treatment I needed, whereas the nurses were a wee bit more personal. They would ask how you felt and ask how many kids you had and did you miss them and things like that. Things that did matter to you. But doctors were very clinical about it.

I was running about and my head was shaved and I was a scary sight. There were people who seen me in the street and crossed over to the other side because they were scared. But what they didn't know was that I was every bit as much scared of them. Maybe more than they were of me. I remember attending Alexander Day Hospital, and it was a doctor who came in one day, and said, 'We don't think you're suffering from depression' and I said, 'Is that right. Well then, can you tell me what it is?' He said, 'We think you're just a very unhappy person.' Now, this was a psychiatrist who said that to me. So I just got up and walked out because I could feel that whole anger – twenty-two years of unhappiness, and he was telling me I hadn't got depression. My father's death had the effect it had on me and I was treating everybody that was close to me like shit – I wasn't a great father to my kids but that was because I was dreadfully unhappy. So, I just said to myself after that, 'You're going to have to start dealing with this yourself.'

But it got a lot worse. I ended up living in two homeless hostels, drinking, taking tablets and going down into the town shoplifting. I wasn't eating anything and I'd lost a lot of weight. I just went up to Shaftesbury Square one day and I knocked the door and the nurse brought me in. I said, 'Look, can you help me, I really need help and I've nobody else to turn to.' She said, 'Well, if you can go away and stay off the drink for a week we'll admit you.' So, I went away and I stayed off the drink for a week. When I came back she says, 'I shouldn't have really told you we could admit you because we haven't got a bed for you, you're going to have to wait another week.' That was devastating. I felt like heading for the nearest pub, but I didn't. I was able to stay off it for another week and then they did admit me.

They put me through a course of vitamin injections to build my weight back up and I started meeting other people, just people that were a victim of circumstances, like myself. I felt better. I was able to remove all the crutches I was leaning on. It was a struggle, the first six or seven weeks was a struggle. It got a bit easier after that because I'd met people and we were going out together, so we were leaning on each other, supporting each other. That was the lowest point ever in my life that I ever actually found the strength to walk in, and ask somebody to help me. I couldn't go on any more. Once it was out, once it was said, I couldn't take it back.

There was somebody that did help me. I had a wee priest that came in to see me. I talked about everything, you know, and he was brilliant. He was crying with me and he was laughing with me too. It was just like sitting talking to a mate. I felt that comfortable with him. After that I ran into my wife again. We had been separated for a while and then we got back together. Things haven't been too bad since then.

I find it hard to concentrate. At the moment I could be working and bringing in an extra few pounds, but it's not laziness, it's just I find it hard to concentrate on things and pressure gets to me very easy. I would panic, but I'd be able to contain it but it would have an effect on me later. The stress of having to contain it and handle it, I would just feel worthless. I have a GP who is brilliant. I really like him. He's a very straight, abrupt person, some people would probably say an ignorant man, but I like somebody who is going to say to me, 'Look, this is the way it is, you done that and it's wrong. Don't do it again, try this.' He would take the time to sit and say, 'How's the drinking going? About your relationship, how's that going?'

I don't think I'll ever put it behind me because it made too much of an impact on my life for me ever to be able to bury it and put it to rest for good. I know for a fact that there's going to be times when I'm going to be depressed; there is going to be times when I'm going to be hard to live with. I know that for a fact, because I've been on the swings and roundabouts that long that I know it's coming round. But hopefully it takes longer each time to come round. As for drugs and prescriptions, well, I don't get them now. They aren't allowed to give me anything.

My father and me were just starting to get to know one another again, because I hadn't seen him for a lot of years, and my mother and him were starting to talk again. There was talk of them getting back together, spending their later years together. Then a wee simple insignificant thing happened. They had an argument and I remember I give him a mouthful, and called him a few expletives and that was the last I seen of him which made it even worse. Because it was three days after that he was killed. Murdered.

I was on a massive guilt trip because I know in my heart that, had he not been murdered, we would probably have been good mates now. We would probably be able to sit and have a pint in the local pub and talk. And he'd be able to see his grandchildren, and they would have the benefit of having him too. All them things go through your head. But, as I say, it's all ifs, buts and maybes. If somebody said to me, 'You can turn the clock back twenty-two years and change whatever you want', I wouldn't change a thing. I like the person that I am now. I'm a sensitive person; I'm very compassionate. I do feel for people, whether they are Protestant or Catholic.

If what's happened to me hadn't happened to me I wouldn't be the person that I am now. Anytime I was knocked down I seemed to find that wee extra bit of strength to get back up again. Where it came from, I don't know, but I suppose that's human nature. It's a survival instinct thing, and we're all capable of it. But I wouldn't change anything.

12   'I don't ask God for anything'

Jolene McAllister was interviewed in her home in Ardoyne, North Belfast in February 1997. At the age of eleven she witnessed her aunt being shot dead in cross-fire between the security forces and Republican paramilitaries. Two years later, she witnessed her cousin being killed in her home. Some time later, her brother was killed in a Republican paramilitary feud.

Well, I'm fifteen now, and I was with my aunt whenever [i.e. when] she was killed in Flax Street. We'd just walked round the corner and there was a whole lot of shots fired and my aunt was shot. There was a fella beside her and he was shot too. Then, over in my house two years ago, the old house round the Crumlin Road, the UVF came into my house and killed my cousin.

I was there with my wee brothers and my mummy. It was my eleventh birthday. When they shot my aunt I was linking [arms with] her. [It was] The IRA. I ... my head was so blank and I got up and I run up to the house. My mummy had heard it was her other sister, Mary. And I told her it was [her sister] Isobel – that I was with her.

She went on down to the hospital. She didn't realise about me being with her [sister]. So, I left and went round to my aunt's and she phoned the doctor for me. And the doctor gave me tablets to calm me down. That was it really.

I don't know what was going through my head. I'm not on the tablets now – it was just for that day. I don't think tablets help you really.

I wouldn't go out. I was too scared. I stayed in the house for weeks. I wouldn't go to school or nothing. Then, I started walking up and down to the shop and I would go down to my aunt's. Then, I started going out again couple of months after that.

Then, I was going to school, but I had to walk past where she was killed to get to school. That stopped me from going to school again, so it did, but I went out for a while.

I just kept getting big flashes through my head [when I went past the place where it happened] about what happened. Now and

12. Isobel Leylands, aunt of Jolene McAllister. This picture was taken shortly before she was killed in 1992. Family photograph

again, I would get them. If I sit and think I would get them. And I wouldn't walk past it no more. I walk past it now, like so I do, because I'm used to it, but I wouldn't walk past it then.

You can just see them falling to the ground. That's the kind of flashes I would get – just see her falling to the ground. Then, I get up and walk out. I don't – I can't sit and think about anything like that. I would go shaky, so I would. It's dreams I have. I start sweating. I can't really sleep. There are times I've sat down here, all night. I wouldn't sleep because it's the dreams. The dreams annoy me. They wake me up in the middle of the night. They annoy me. They scare me.

I used to go to a doctor over in the Royal, a Doctor M., and I didn't like her, so I got Doctor C. and I liked her. She was brilliant. Now she's away, I've to go back to M., but I don't want to go back, so I haven't been there in near two years.

What is the difference between Dr M. and Dr C.?

Dr M. just keeps repeating the same thing, the same thing. Dr C. would give you something to do, and then spoke to you.

I got threw out of that school so I did. My behaviour just went wild. I was never cheeky or anything, but now, I am, and they threw me out. I'm nasty. If I don't get what I want I start moaning. I was never like that. I've always said, there's a quare change in me.

What did I get up to in school? Well, in the other school, I was always running about and fighting, with the teachers, throwing things and all. It was just, I was always tired, always trying to go to sleep. Then, the teachers would shout, and then I'd throw the books across the classroom, and then I'd do no work. That's how it all started. Then, at break time, I'd run up and down the corridors throwing bottles at the teachers – plastic bottles – and that was just to get you into trouble. I was never like that at primary school. I never once got a bad report. I was always brilliant.

But the new school I'm in – I like that school, so I do, and I can't be cheeky in it, anyway, because the teacher phones the house. I'd be cheeky still, but not as cheeky as I was over there. They are all good teachers over there; they take time with you. I like it up there. I don't get into trouble in that school because the teachers are good to you, and that there's what I said to my mother. I realised that if you are good to them'uns they'll be good to you. Over [in the other school] they didn't, and that school's scary! I don't like big schools with a whole lot of people in it. There's 260 over there – there's only twenty-two up there.

But at first, whenever I was with my aunt, whenever she was killed, my mummy thought I was acting, you know, to stay off school. But she said, whenever she seen my cousin getting killed, she knows now what I was going through, because she doesn't think anybody would know, unless it's happened to them. She was always saying, 'Go on, get off for school!' I always said, 'No, I don't want to go.' But she made me go, so she did.

Was there anybody at all that was sympathetic, who thought, 'I wonder how Jolene is?'

I don't know really. A wee girl round the street, I was always with her, but I just … it was something I wouldn't talk about. I'd try to forget about it. I think that's the way I went for a while. I'd be sitting and people would be talking to me. It would take me a couple of minutes to click on to what they were saying. I didn't listen – thinking about everything, about what happened.

Well, I don't know, actually, why it happened because they were shooting at the peelers, like, and they just happened to miss and kill my aunt. But I'd love to know who it was, so I would. Because the person that killed my aunt, I could be talking to them, saying, 'Hiya' and all. But if I knew who it was, I wouldn't talk, so I wouldn't, 'cause they shouldn't have been shooting people that were on the streets. They shouldn't have been shooting at all. If it was somebody I knew, I'd be shocked. But sure, it doesn't really matter now, does it, who killed her? It's done.

They're scum, that's all I can say, because they nearly killed me and they nearly killed a six-year-old child as well. If we hadn't been pushed out of the road like we were, sure, we would have been dead too. That would have been four people killed, because the other man that was shot, he's still alive. I said to my mummy, 'Why was it not me, instead of her?' Because she was going home that night, so she was. My mummy says, 'That's just the way things go.'

I'm very bad tempered and my brother and me are always fighting. He could be sitting there watching TV, and he dances round you. And used to be he could do that for ages and ages before that annoyed me – but as soon as he does it once, I'll get up and hit him … and he's older than me. He's 17. He annoys me. It's like, if I'm walking down the street and the wee lads are kicking the ball and the ball hits me, I'd hit the person that kicked the ball. All that stuff annoys me, so it does.

I lost a brother seven months ago. He was my best brother. He was dead close to me that one. He was killed. The INLA shot him in Turf Lodge, seven months ago. Then, his girl[friend] had his wee child two weeks after he was killed. That wrecked me so it did. It's wrecked our whole family because he was the special one out of the whole family. I don't know what it was … it's not as if he was stupid or anything, but he would do stupid things. He wasn't all there, like. And I don't know … everybody loved him.

Now, he got two beatings so he did, and he was paralysed in the arm by what they call the Provies. It was the Provies that beat him, and my brother spoke to them. He was one that couldn't hold a grudge. He always spoke to the person that beat him. He knew who beat him. But all he said, 'Right!', you know, that there? But he wouldn't stand for a full conversation. I don't know what it was. He was just the special one out of our whole family, so he was.

That wrecked me, so it did. It wrecked everybody, not only me – everybody. Do you know, even, people out in the street that wouldn't have liked him whenever he was alive, but always said he was a good child. He always did everything for you. If he'd no money, he'd run miles to get money for you. He was that type of person. It wrecked everybody, so it did. And you know, like, people say to me, 'How's your mummy after [brother's name] was killed?' I wouldn't answer, I'd walk away. And because ... I don't know ... I just couldn't talk about him. People, I just think, are being nosy. People like that, I wouldn't talk to.

I've got even cheekier and nastier, so I have. I don't know, it's just all wee dopey things – telling my ma to shut up and I hate her, she's a fat bitch, and all that there – all that kind of stuff. I don't mean it. It just comes out. If I go to school, I said to mummy, 'Why is my jeans not drying for me?' And, if they aren't dry whenever I put them on, I'll crack up. Or, if she won't give me money, I crack up. Or, if I'm asked to go a message and I don't want to go, I crack up and start screaming and slamming doors. Yet, my mummy gets me off for school. I have to get up because the bus collects me, but it wrecks me getting up, and she'll say to me, 'Do you not want your breakfast?' And I'll be dead cheeky to her, even when she is being nice to me.

I feel sorry for her, so I do, because she's been strong with all us, because it's wrecked my mummy. My brothers annoy her. My second brother, he really annoys her. He gets out and gets himself into trouble and all, so he does. He was never, ever cheeky. We've all just changed and I don't know why. He has changed from our brother was killed. My mummy's changed. I know she's changed, but I can't exactly see what way she's changed. She's changed in all different ways.

I get out of school on a half day on Friday, and there'd be times that my daddy wouldn't be in and the child [her dead brother's child] would be over. And she'd lift the child up to the photo, and all, and say, 'There's my son, there's your dad', you know, talk to the photo. She never ever did that, not even with her mummy's photo. At night, she does not sleep. You'd be lying in bed and you'd hear the crying, then she puts out her fag and then lights up another one. All she does is smoke.

She stopped darts whenever my cousin was killed. She used to go to bingo and all, now she'll not go out at all. She'll go out on a Monday night to the Trauma meeting [a self-help group] and on a Saturday night to the bingo. My wee friend and me would babysit for her. Now she doesn't go out at all really. Well I can't say to her, 'Mummy, go out!' because if you say, 'Mummy, go out!' she'll say, 'I'm fed up. I'm not going out.' But, she would have to go out then, to make herself happy, wouldn't she?

Will I tell you what happened about my cousin? My friend and me, a wee girl that stays with me at the weekend, walked in the door and she went into the living room. And I went in and says to mummy, 'Is the dinner ready?' She said, 'It's nearly ready now!' And I went back into the living room, and I'd heard our cousin's voice. He was stupid, but you'd have got a laugh out of him. He'd come in and say all this stuff that wasn't true, just to get money off you. He said to my mummy, 'Some man's looking me on Friday night for a job, and I need money for petrol.' But it was really for a bet. I said, 'There's our cousin! Come on out and we'll get a laugh!' And she said, 'Well, I'm watching this [on television]!' And I went out and we were all standing there talking.

My Mummy said to me, 'Did you shut the front door?' And I said, 'No!' She said, 'Go out and shut it!' I said, 'Hold on. I'll shut it in a minute!' And she said, 'Get out and shut it now!' And I said, 'No! I'm not going out to shut it!' Our child had fallen – my wee brother. He'd fell, and my cousin lifted him up and put him on his shoulders, and went to walk out the back to my daddy and my cousin's brother.

This fella came in [the front door] and he shouted, 'Yo!' And we turned round, and he'd shot my cousin in the neck. My wee brother fell off [my cousin's shoulders] and hit his head off a gas barrel, and my wee brother was just lying there. My cousin went down on his two knees and he got back up again. He went to run for your man, but he slipped in his own blood. And the man said to him, 'Die, you Fenian bastard!' And he shot him another twice in the head – another two times in the head – and just walked out.

I just stood there and looked at him. I froze – I couldn't do nothing. And my mother was on the ground. She'd collapsed. She didn't know what was happening. And then she got up and she run. My daddy run in and then run out again, and I was still standing there. Then I walked out and seen my mummy. She'd collapsed over my cousin's car. And I walked into the kitchen, and my wee brother was lying over my cousin, all full of blood. My wee brother was only two.

I just didn't want to talk to anybody. And then my mummy's sister came round and she started bringing us up to the graveyard, bringing me up to the graveyard every Sunday. And then going up to the graveyard made you think back. 'Why didn't I shut our front door, and all, whenever I was told to?' Like my daddy, my cousin and my brother, if they had of been all in that kitchen, I'm sure they would have been dead too. There was nothing they could have done, because your man had a gun.

And the wee girl that stays with me at the weekends, your man went into her first and booted the legs of her – left all big bruises on her legs and told her to get out of the house, that he had something to do. She walked in behind him. And she stopped behind him, while he was shooting my cousin.

My Mummy had a chip pan in her hand and it was really bubbling. And she says, 'Why didn't I throw it?' And I said, 'Why didn't I run past him before the peelers?' and my other brother said, 'If I had've been up the stairs, I would have come down and lifted the [poker] and hit him on the back of the head with it!' And then, I just clicked on and said, 'But sure, you think them things after it, don't you?'

Now the peelers set it up. The peelers caused all that, because my brother was lifted one day, so he was. He was lifted for a murder of an Orangeman, but he didn't do it, and the peelers knew it. He was brought into Castlereagh [Interrogation Centre], and because he was getting out, because they knew that he didn't do it, they says that [a named person] would be out to see him. They'd give him a week to two weeks and then [a named person] would be out to see him.

My brother got out that Monday, and [the named person] came in to our house and killed my cousin that Thursday. As I ran out to the street, there were two peelers at the bottom of the street to make sure they got away all right. So the peelers set it up. About seven months before that, the peelers had told my cousin that he was going to get killed as well. They've just something against our family and they never, ever liked them.

It's just the way [my aunt] was. It wrecked me, so it did. That stopped me from going out for a while. We had to move out of our house into a two-bedroom house, and there was the whole family there. We were all squashed. The house was all messed up with all our stuff going into it. Then, we got this house, and this house was like a dump. My ma was steaming these walls and they fell down on top of us, and everything was just going wrong for us. My daddy loved that house round there – he didn't want to move out of it – but the peelers said to my mother, it would be good advice to move out because they'd be back, because they didn't get my brother. They were really out for my brother.

Most of my family is here, all my aunts and uncles and all, and they all live close. We were going to move to Cork, me and my mummy and all, but then I said, I didn't want to move and mummy said she didn't want to move either, because all her brothers and sisters were here. So we didn't move. My daddy did want to move, but he didn't want to move really because his mummy lives here. I don't want to move out of here. I want to stay here in this house because I think we're closed in this way, you know, with that big wall there. But that big wall's going away, anyway. They're building a park there.

I was never out of Mass. Now, I wouldn't even go to Mass. The only time I've been to that Mass is at wakes, or christenings ... that's been it. That's been from my aunt was killed. I haven't been to Mass since she was killed. It bores me now. It used to be, every time the chapel bells ring, I would run over. But now, I wouldn't even think about going to Mass. I think when I say my prayers at night that's my Mass over and done with. I don't ask God for anything.

Do you hear the way people say about the cease-fires broke, and then they're thinking about a new one? I don't want the cease-fire to break. Then that means all the people getting kneecapped. That's what my brother got – two punishment beatings, with iron bars stuck through his arms and legs. He was only sixteen and eighteen [the second time]. They tied him up and put a paper brown bag over his head after they did it, and then threw him over a back wall.

His mate's still joyriding now, for years and years and years, and he never got beat once. I don't think they should be doing that, especially paralysing him and all that. That's not right. He was paralysed in his arm. He could move his fingers, but he couldn't straighten them and use them. He had all big scars around his legs and arms. But yet, he spoke to people that beat him, so he would have.

I don't like Brits and the peelers. There are times I do like them about – whenever it's too quiet and you think that something is going to happen. But you see, walking about the streets shouting at people and just beating people for nothing, I don't like that. They shouldn't do that. It's only making people bitter against them.

13 'Just me and the kids'

Bel McGuiness was interviewed in March 1997 in Bawnmore, Greencastle, a Catholic enclave in North Belfast. Her husband was killed by a plastic bullet in August 1982 and she is now very involved in Greencastle Women's Group, a self-help group in the area.

Well, effects of the Troubles. I was widowed in August 1981 when Peter was shot dead by a plastic bullet. I was left with five children. The oldest was thirteen going on fourteen, and the youngest was almost eight. Actually his eighth birthday was the week after his father's death. It was a hard time for him because the kids look forward to their birthday party. They wouldn't have big massive parties but you would have had a wee family thing together. I'll always remember that for him.

It was internment night. The 8th August going into the 9th, 1981. It was a Saturday night and they always had a bonfire. So I used to take the oldest girl up just to see the bonfire, and we would have stood at the bottom of the hill and stayed there for maybe half an hour or so and I'd of brought her back down again. This particular night I had been working. I'd just started working in the club, so I'd done a Saturday night in it waitressing. I thought I heard in the distance bangs and I'd seen the bottom of the Mill Road where the police were. They were firing plastic bullets. Although I heard these bangs I didn't know what it was about. So we went on into the house and we had our tea, and Margaret went on to bed. So the next thing more of a crowd had gathered and more petrol bombs and I went out. There was this tree, the tree is still there yet, and what I was frightened of was the petrol bomb hitting that tree.

The guy that lived next door to me, he took me by the arm and says, 'Come on' because the police came on the scene. So I thought Peter and Barney were coming behind us and I just got into the hall when there was a bang, a flash, and the next thing Peter came running up the hill and just shouts, 'Bel I've been hit.' So he went to get on to the chair and I couldn't see where he'd been hit, you know. He'd been shot right in the chest you see. There was no

13. Bel McGuiness pictured outside the office of the Greencastle Women's
Group in December 1998. Photograph: Marie Smyth

blood and I couldn't understand. So I panicked. There were a few
people about. An ambulance was on the way up the Shore Road
anyway so they stopped it. One of the ambulance men got out and
opened Peter's T-shirt and he started working with him. He was
just out on the floor and all you could hear was bones cracking. The
whole breast-plate had been pushed right back with the force of it
and there was nothing they could do.

So they sent for the priest and it happened to be my cousin. My cousin is a priest. He repeated the last rites and sat down to talk to me and the next thing there was a knock at the door and it was two plain clothes policemen to take a statement. These detectives came in and I was talking to them anyway just more or less about what had happened. So I think somebody must have said then enough is enough because I was rambling. I thought at the time that I was quite sane, quite capable of this, and I probably was because I went and I made tea and sandwiches and Peter is lying dead on my floor like. This was shortly after two on the Sunday morning. I think it was something like half four before they came to take the body away. He'd been lying for about two hours, lying on my floor with people in over walking over the top of him. It was a wee small kitchen.

They took Peter out in a black bag. That was the first time I'd ever seen anything like that. They put him in and zipped it round him and carried him out. He wasn't involved in any petrol bombing or anything like that. He was cleared. The inquest was something like over a year afterwards, a year and three months afterwards. I'd to go through all that again. He was cleared of any criminal activities.

Of course I never got any compensation for Peter because he wasn't working, so they didn't think he or I was entitled to anything. I don't think I even got funeral expenses. I don't believe it, because there was a few do's run by the club and the local bingo. I had an insurance policy and you paid what you could afford, but the guy who I knew very well, he says, 'Look can you not up it a wee bit' because you know he was more or less thinking with the Troubles anything can happen at any time and you don't want to be left. I said, 'Aye go ahead' and it was probably another 50p a week or something like that. It was just hard to believe, because it was just through over a month when Peter was shot dead, which meant I got double my premiums. That always sticks in my mind you know, whether it was being mercenary I don't know.

The money went. You were giving the kids treats. How do you make up to the kids for their father not being there, especially under them circumstances? So probably I squandered an awful lot of money, plus I started drinking anyway. I could never work while Peter was alive, so I took on a wee job which was up beside the Dockers club. Drink was easy to have then, it was very accessible. So, it knocked me for six quite truthfully and changed my whole life. Because for somebody who didn't get out much, Peter would have took me out once a month. Him and I would get a babysitter in and we would go out together. But me personally, I didn't get out that much, so it led then to, what do you do with yourself? You've all this money, what do you do?

I probably squandered a terrible lot of it. I moved up into the house which had been my mother's house, with my youngest sister, who was single. I think it was quite a shock to the system. We had great times and her and I got on quite well. She took my oldest one to the town and all on a Saturday. The boys she wasn't so keen on. She liked wee girls, but, she wasn't so keen on the wee lads. The wee lads were too boisterous for her, whereas, she could maybe talk more to the wee girls. She'd no kids of her own so I suppose she didn't have much experience in that way. But I stayed there for about four months.

I always went down and visited my wee house. If I wanted to get into myself a wee bit I sort of took off to my wee house. I would have lit a fire and I just sat on my own. So eventually then, there was a house three doors up, so I moved up in there. It was a better house. There was an electric light and a tap you could turn on and off so there was constant running water. It was quite good, I liked it. I had my own space again, and I could have coped with the kids better. Then the vesting order was out and we all had to move, and that's when I moved into Bawnmore. So we just carried on. I just worked away.

I was working, of course as I say, with easy access to drink, so it ended up I had to have my gall bladder removed. There were holes in it. Quite truthfully it was horrendous, because I ended up in hospital losing part of my body, and getting cut up. I went through a really terrible time with it.

I'd a great daughter. I would start work from 8.30 in the morning and about 2.30/2.45 went to the pub, got the stuff and a taxi home. My daughter run my house and signed the pension books and whatever. She ran my house at fourteen. She has been so supportive, and she had been my crutch in more ways than one. Even yet she would be. But at that time, that child must have been in some hell of a state. She had to see this and put up with it and there was nothing she could do about it. I've gained maybe the experience of knowing the hardships and hopefully can pass them on, whether anyone will listen or not. My past experiences – where I went wrong, well that would be the pitfalls, to avoid the drink. If you want to have a drink, have it, make a special night for it, and keep to it.

You see the grandchildren growing up and you know there's another generation coming up here, let's make the best for them. And with the women's group it can be done. There is real dedication here. Anything for the better.

14   Rough Justice

The interviewee who wishes to remain anonymous was interviewed at his home in Derry Londonderry in April 1997. From the age of thirteen he has been the victim of paramilitary punishment beatings. Over the years he has sustained injuries to almost every one of his limbs and joints and his education and prospects for the future have been damaged.

Well, I've had thirteen punishment beatings, by paramilitaries: iron bars, sledge-hammers and hurley bats. They made you lie on streets, made you lie on a fence, made you run and hide.

I couldn't go near any of my family's houses because paramilitaries told them that if they got me in the house, they would break into the house and do me in – and the people beside me. So I had to keep on trying to dodge them all the time, and then they were getting me, they were battering me and they were coming back at me and saying to me, 'You've twenty-four hours to get out of the country.' Then they turn round and say, 'If you don't go, we're going to shoot you.' And I still wouldn't go. They got me again and they battered me again.

It has happened since I was thirteen up to right up to seventeen. Well, I was getting into wee petty things, like stealing and all that there. If you got caught by the police you were taken to court. And when the courts were done with you, they [the paramilitaries] were after you, so you were getting done two ways. Even in between the court, I used to go to court with crutches, staples down my head, bandaged and everything. The way I looked at it – it wasn't fair that the police got me and took me to court, and I would have to stand in front of the court to get dealt with. And then, when the court punished me, the paramilitaries would get me anyway and give me their punishment.

They want me to leave the country. First time they wanted me to leave the country, I was only thirteen. They took me away for six hours and burnt me with fags. They struck me with a soldering iron bar and made me kneel down for six hours and battered the back of me with a bat, while I had a hood over my head. They

14. Port of Belfast, the departure point for many who leave Northern Ireland. Photograph: Marie Smyth

were threatening to take me and shoot me dead and bury me, and all that there. They said, 'You've three things to pick from: leave the country; kneecapped; or drilled and then shot.' I said I'd leave the country, but I only said that so they'd let me go. And then I had to keep hiding from them.

So from I was thirteen, everything that was getting done [in the neighbourhood] they were coming back and blaming me for it, and I wasn't here half the times that the things were being done. So that's the way they were working. They wanted to see me out of the country for good. That's the way they had their grudge.

I got a name – for young fellas who looked up to me when I was running from the IRA and not leaving the country – so when they started getting into trouble, they started to finish it. So, the IRA was blaming me and saying it was my fault because if I hadn't of stood up to them, no one would have stood up. There was nobody stood up to them before me.

They say I was the ringleader of all the hoods so they [the hoods] are all looking up to me, and they are going to follow suit. That wasn't fair. They stuck a label on my back. Every time you see him, just beat him. That was more or less the way they were putting it. I was just like any other young fella going through a bad patch. Like, when you are growing up, you get into a bit of trouble. But they left me in that much trouble that I couldn't get out of. It was their fault. They left me that I'd nowhere to run, nowhere to hide but hide and fight.

Half the time I was standing in the rain and fights, the rain dropping down round me, not a bit of grub into me for two and a half days. I was afraid to come back here, because if they knew I was coming back, they were waiting. It was like twenty-four hours round the clock. I had to watch my back. I had to keep looking over my shoulder when I was walking over the street. I couldn't walk, I had to run and make sure I got out of alley-ways, because that's where they would mostly get me. They were waiting in alley-ways and I was walking through and they were holding on to me.

I was sitting on the wall and these four boys came over to me with sledge-hammers and said, 'We're with the Provisional IRA', and started to whale into me. I asked them for a reason, and they just battered me and told me to get out of the country. They said they were going to shoot me dead. Then, I said I wasn't going and they says, 'Right you're defying us again, so you'll stand and take your lickin'.'

Where was I going to go to? This is my country. I was brought up here. Why should I leave, just because they are shouting? Defying them – that was their main reason. I was running around – I would write up a house or a wall or something. I would steal things out of the back of vans, or I would break into a couple of places. But, I didn't go breaking into places until they started to torture me, and then I had to break in. It was the only way I could have survived because I couldn't come near the area. I had to break in to try and get food, to keep me going on the run from them'uns.

I was so afraid. I was putting my whole family … even my wee sisters, they seen me getting dragged out and dragged down the stairs. Me da also seen me. My wee sister, she was only young at the time, they booted me down the stairs in front of her. They told me to get out the door. They took me into the sitting room and brought my girlfriend in, turned her head and said, 'Watch what you are going with', and then they whaled into me, in front of her. She sat and watched everything, and that split me and her up. She couldn't even walk the streets with me because she knew what was going to happen. They more or less told her either to get away from me or you're going to see more of this here. So she called it quits, she wasn't going through that again.

I would sneak into my granny's. I would be up at five or six in the morning – until it was daylight – and get a sleep in her house. I couldn't go back the next night in case they were watching there, so I would sneak into other people's houses, friends' houses even, and stay in their's. I've seen me sleeping in the back of people's hedge with a blanket around me and it pissing down with rain. It had to be done, because if they had've got me, they were for crippling me, or putting me down a hole. So it was either keep running, or that's the way it went.

And still now to this day, when it gets dark, my nerves would just completely shatter. And when I am walking anywhere, I just always watch over me shoulder. If somebody sees, and the Provos are about, I get it in my head straight away that they are looking for me and I just don't move until I hear they are away. I just stay and watch, keep watching.

I wouldn't have slept at night. When we all slept in the room for about three years, one of us had to stay awake all the time to see a paramilitary. It was a cert. Seven nights a week they were at this door – every night of the week. They were up wrecking the house looking for me. The boys were coming in with sledge-hammers, with cullens, with guns, and they had four houses under watch with all different units. This house, my granny's house, my ma's friend's house and my brother's girlfriend's house – all in the one night all looking for me – all at the same time, too. They thought I had to be in one of these houses. But I was in the attic up the stairs and I'd to stay out the next morning, and then I had to get out of there and get hiding again ... back on to the streets then, just hiding from them all the time. That's the way it went.

Well I got thirty-five stitches in my leg and my wrist. I was bandaged from my ankles right up. My elbow was broke, my wrist was broke and I'd fractured kneecaps, swollen kneecaps, my ankles were broke and I'd slices all over my arms and legs and my head. I think my eyes were sitting out, and my nose got broke. They just didn't care where they hit me. They just went at me, hoping that they would maim me for life or half kill me – leave me for dead. They just didn't care.

All my bones bother me. I can't walk a distance, but I have to stop. All my bones are playing up and the doctor says it's guaranteed I'm going to get arthritis. I am only nineteen, and he reckons before I'm twenty-five, I'm going to be suffering with arthritis. I'm only starting to sleep well now, this past while. I used to stay up all night and sleep that day and then, even if I came out at daytime, I wasn't safe. They didn't care. Even if it was daytime, they were coming for me. So, I wasn't sleeping. There were times I wasn't sleeping for four days. I got a couple of hours' sleep and I was shattered. I was walking round in circles. I didn't know what to do. I don't go to sleep until about four or five in the morning. I go over and sit in the garage, or watch the TV. Just waiting for daylight so I can get some sleep.

It spoilt everything for me – spoilt everything. I can't read and I can't write. I lost everything because of that. I was doing all right at school, but when that came, that was when I left school. I was taken to court for leaving school. I was in school one day maybe out of four months because of them'uns, and you couldn't turn round and say to the school that paramilitaries are going to come to my family. You have to watch what you say to people.

The only people I got help from were my own family, that's it. I got no help at all. I had a probation officer, but there's not much they can do. I mean, they can help during the day, but after that, they finish at 5.30 p.m. There's nothing else they can do. You're on your own from then on, so you are left to stand and face it all.

I got £2,500 in compensation. That's what I got for the lot. I was gutted when I heard what I got. I should have never got the beatings, anyway, and I should have been entitled to a lot more than that there. The beatings I got, I was left ill for weeks and weeks. I got beat with iron bars, so I couldn't even walk for six weeks. I had to sit in a chair for two weeks nearly. If I wanted to go to the toilet, they had to carry me, because my legs were just mangled from under me.

They burnt this house and that was their downfall then. If they hadn't burnt this house – and this is fact – I would have been in a wheelchair now, or in a cemetery, and that is guaranteed. They couldn't get me, so they took it out on the house and I think it was two nights before, they marched up and down there, a big guy in a mask shot a single shot up into the house. The men burnt the house, but when we went to the head of the organisation they came out with a load of crap. The order wasn't put out to burn the house, yet their men burnt the house. Their excuse was that they were drunk, but they weren't planning to burn the house. That makes it OK for them'uns, but if it had of been me and I burnt a house, they'd shoot me and leave me in an alley-way.

I went to the Sinn Fein Centre and they had witnesses there. They never let me see them, but I heard your man saying to the Sinn Fein man, 'It's not him, it's definitely not him.' He's too well built for it, or he's too small for it.' And the other boy kept saying to him, 'Are you sure? It might be him. Take a good look.' They were trying to put words into your man's mouth. But your man was saying, 'It's not him.' And the Sinn Fein man said, 'Well, that's it.' They knew they'd made a fatal mistake. There were two squads of them. They were actually fighting each other over the mistakes that they made.

Now, I'm on the sick for life. All my bones are all wrecked. I can't work because of my elbow. The bone was split like that there, and they couldn't operate. I've got asthma and other things. I go to snooker to pass the time, and we'd play a game of cards or go to bingo. I don't even go up the town to the pubs because, I know rightly, the minute I'd walked in, it's all Provos in it. It's the paramilitaries that run them. I don't go near them. I just stay away altogether.

It was the Provos have wrecked my life. If they hadn't been in this country, this country would have been a great country. As soon as they took over, they maimed more people, even their own people. The people that done this to me are definitely scumbags. They are bringing up families of their own, but whenever their sons or daughters get into trouble, because they are in the IRA, they'll get nothing done to them. They'll get away with murder. They'll not be classed as hoods. They'll just turn round and say, 'My son has just gone off the rail for a wee while. I'll put him back right.' And they'll bring their sons up to run around, 'My da's in the Provos. You hit me, and my da will get you shot.'

That's the way you do things in this country. If somebody comes up and whacks you, 'Go on, hit me back, I'm a member of the IRA. I'll get you shot.' What can you do? You can't lift your hand back. Personally speaking, I hate them. I can't stand them. I should have told them when they were battering me, 'All you are is scumbags.' I don't care, because they wanted me out of my own country. I was no angel. I would get into trouble.

I got sent to St Patrick's Training School and I think that was the thing that more or less saved me. I was never up in court for anything serious, it was all just wee petty things. I didn't get any big sentence for them. It was like a contest to see who could take me out first and that was the way they were playing it. I used to hang around with young fellas, so they were taking me out to batter me, to show them, 'You step out of line you are going to get what he got!' So, they used me as a scapegoat to batter every time they wanted to teach somebody right from wrong.

Every time they went to somebody high, somebody with authority, they were telling them ones a story to put them off. They let the paramilitaries off again and then, when they went back, 'I don't know how that happened. We'll check it out', and then another would come along. They are all liars, and I would stand up to them and tell them what they are. I said, 'I've told you, I'm not leaving the country.' And if they came back tonight to shoot me dead if I didn't go, I'd stand and I'd let them shoot me because they've ruined my life anyway. I'm all nerves and I can't go out anymore because the fear never leaves you.

I still get nightmares to this day, and I'd waken the whole house with the roaring I do, because when you sleep, everything just flashes back in front of you. I'm allright now, but to this day, I still watch my back, I still look over my shoulder. When I'm walking through alley-ways, I walk really slow. If there is anybody standing there, I turn and go the other way straight away. No way will I face them. I wouldn't go down an alley-way.

I did get a bit of peace in St Patrick's [Training School]. I'd a bit of peace to myself. I was all right in there. I said, 'Can I take a weekend down?' They said it was OK. They [the paramilitaries] came in here the Monday night, with batons and guns, looking for me but I was away back to St Pat's. Then they changed their minds at St Pat's – no weekends at all, so that was that. I hoofed it from St Pat's and came back to Derry. I stayed on the run from St Pat's until the police got me and took me back. Then St Pat's had to release me because my time was up. I only got a Training [School] Order you see, so I only did six months and they let me go.

My da took a couple of overdoses because of it. He's an alcoholic. He just didn't want to face it sober, so all he did was try and hide it away, but he knew it wasn't going away. He wasn't going to stand and watch it happen sober, so he had a drink. Just drink, drink, drink. He's all right now, but that's what they [the paramilitaries] do to you. They wreck your nerves and they know they do, with their threats and their guns.

Cease-fires? Sure when they called a cease-fire, a cease-fire wasn't on here. They are still running around doing people. They are still doing their punishment beatings. So, I can't see how that is a cease-fire. A cease-fire is everything called off, not just bombings and shootings. Even when they called a cease-fire, they were still carrying out kneecappings and punishment beatings. When the cease-fires were called, the beatings were harder and did more damage.

My brother and my two other sisters all went to a counsellor over it. That was the reason why, there was no other reason. My sister was up in Belfast yesterday. They took her up for a brain scan to try and find out what is behind her head. Her doctor knows it, we know it, but they are trying to find out what really sparked her.

People my age, they definitely haven't got anything. My brother is only twenty-three, and he hates this country. He went to England to try and have a better life because this country is just ripped to bits. He likes it over there. He has a better life. He's not running around hearing about people getting shot dead, left for dead.

If I wanted to go to England or anywhere, even next week, I would go, but I would be saying, 'It's me, myself, telling me to go.' Nobody is telling me to go! Nobody is making me go! And I would be happy enough at that. I'd be able to go on holiday or whatever. I wouldn't go on their say so and on their terms. I just think to myself, 'Get up, and get away. Get away from Ireland and see what I can do with my life.'

There are days when it comes into my head all the time. I'm still thinking very strong about it and I'm attempting to pick up the pieces of what they destroyed. Thinking about it and doing it are two different things. Maybe some day I will take the chance and get up and go.

Conclusions

Our knowledge of all periods in human history is necessarily partial, based on written records that are made at the time or soon afterwards, sometimes the memories of participants, and the stories that are told. Most historical knowledge from written sources lacks the texture and depth that the untold stories can add. This is as true of Northern Ireland's Troubles as of the conflict in the Middle East, the First or Second World War, or any other set of events. Whilst some of the personal accounts in this book have been collected before, they were edited by hands other than those of the storyteller. Here, in their own albeit edited words, people tell their stories. Other accounts appear here for the first time.

E.P. Thompson's (1963) early conceptualisation history was of two kinds: history from above, and history from below, history from the point of view of the powerful compared to the rather different and less well represented perspective of the less powerful. More recent insights have offered analysis of the multiple and diverse nature of human experience, and the tendency for history to omit the accounts of some lives and to focus on the famous, infamous and powerful individuals and groups. The accounts we have collected are those of less well known – for the most part working-class – people whose lives have been affected by the Troubles, and who responded in various ways to the events that altered their lives. The challenge to the outsider is to attend to the complexities of experience of those who have lived in communities experiencing ongoing armed conflict, imposing our concerns or interpretations on their stories. These are the experts on their own lives and experiences, and if we, the outsiders, listen carefully, we might learn more about how they experience their world, in so doing learn about ourselves, and therefore learn more about the world itself.

As is apparent from the accounts in this book, the Troubles have not been experienced as a single event, but rather as a series of events over a period of years, or over a lifetime. Part of the individual difference in response to a particular event may be related to the person's previous experience of *other* Troubles events. Over the decades of the Troubles individuals, particularly those in areas worst affected by the Troubles, often have had multiple experiences of Troubles-related injury, loss and bereavement, as is apparent from the accounts in this book. Many geographical communities – in North and West Belfast, in Derry City and in the border regions – have seen many incidents, on almost a daily basis over a period of decades. The same is true of some communities of interest, such as the local security forces.

The likely impact of an event in the Troubles is clearly affected by the person's, the family's or the community's proximity to the event. The greater the proximity, the larger the impact is likely to be. Proximity, however, is not simply a matter of spatial arrangement. Proximity may also be relational, or temporal. An event can be close in time to an individual (it happened in the last hour) but spatially distant (in another town) and relationally distant (people I do not know and cannot sympathise with). If the relational proximity increases, the likely impact also dramatically increases. If the people involved are people I can identify with, or people related to me, or even people in my own family, then the impact is more likely to be traumatic. A child who was not born when his/her father was killed will still be impacted by the death because of the relational proximity, through the effect on the family, living group, or community, even though in temporal terms that child was 'distant' from the event.

The impact of any event must be seen not only in relation to the characteristics of the event itself, but also in relation to the impact of other events that may have rendered the individual or community vulnerable. In interview, it was noticeable how individuals would under-report certain experiences of the Troubles, and would only 'remember' them, and confirm their experience of them, when prompted. Other events, which were closer, geographically, in time or relationally, take precedence. As a result, other experiences are 'displaced' in consciousness – almost as if the individual has a capacity for consciousness of, or remembering, a certain number of intense experiences. When that capacity is exceeded, they 'forget' – or at least no longer spontaneously call to mind – earlier events, events that previously they may have regarded as very intense or potent.

Very few older interviewees spontaneously mentioned being stopped and searched by the security forces as an experience of the Troubles *per se,* yet visitors to Northern Ireland go home and recount such tales with horror, since they represent their position of greatest proximity to the trauma of the Troubles. In terms of the wider Northern Ireland society, this would suggest that of the myriad events that have happened, people no longer think about spontaneously or even remember many of them without prompting, because they have been displaced in their perceptual field by more intense or closer events. This does not mean that individuals were unaffected by events they no longer call to mind, but rather that these events have moved down their individual perceptual hierarchy of events that have affected them.

In reviewing the interview data, it struck us that, as people accumulate more and more experience of the Troubles, their organisation of these experiences in memory might resemble such a hierarchy, with recent, direct personal or more powerful /unusual experiences at the top of the hierarchy and past experiences, less powerful/unusual or experiences of others ranking lower on the hierarchy. Perhaps in giving accounts of the Troubles, the 'lower order' experiences come to be taken for granted and are less frequently mentioned in these accounts of experiences of the Troubles. This could also be due to people habituating to some experiences, such as hearing helicopters overhead, so that after a period of constant exposure to the experience, it is regarded as 'normal' and therefore not worth reporting. This may have been compounded in our interviews, by the fact that both interviewers were 'insiders' to some extent, both being from Northern Ireland. Perhaps assumptions were made by our informants that certain experiences that one might report to an outsider need not be reported to us, since they were taken for granted, 'normal', or of too low an order.

As a result of doing various interviews over the past few years in Northern Ireland, together with the impact of doing other analysis of the impact of the Troubles, it seems that there are a series of versions of realities in relation to the Troubles. Whereas the image of the outsider might be that Northern Ireland is suffused with the experience and effects of armed conflict, in fact, the Troubles have had most of their impact in relatively small concentrated geographical areas, and usually within poorer communities. There are many regions of Northern Ireland which have been relatively slightly affected by the Troubles. It is as if there are two or maybe three 'worlds' in Northern Ireland in relation to the Troubles.

In the dominant world, the world of business, higher education, the media, people in positions of relative autonomy do not talk about their personal experiences of the Troubles. This world operates on a set of assumptions about the Troubles: that the Troubles affect other people, not one's close associates, family or friends; that the people affected by the Troubles have chosen to be involved in politics or made some other choice that then placed them in a position in which the Troubles then affected them. In short, this world operates within a framework of denial of and dissociation from the effects of the Troubles. This denial and dissociation is partly determined by social class, given that over-whelmingly, and with few exceptions, it is the poorest communities that have been most drastically and deeply affected by the Troubles. Those exceptional individuals who do inhabit this world and who do have personal experience of the Troubles tend not to disclose that experience because it would be 'inappropriate' and because to do so might jeopardise one's position or social standing in this world.

There is a further and more extreme tier to this world, where to raise the subject of the Troubles is perceived as socially gauche, like talking about money or religion. To raise the subject within certain social circles in Northern Ireland is to provoke anger and active resistance. There are various morals of these dominant worlds: 'If you are bereaved, injured or otherwise affected by the Troubles, it is because you attracted those events to yourself by your behaviour, attitudes or affiliations.' This, of course, means that two myths can proliferate: that 'respectable' people are safe; and that those who have been hurt – with few carefully defined exceptions – brought it on themselves.

People who inhabit this world have little, if any, direct experience of the Troubles, they live in areas that have remained virtually untouched by the violence, and work in jobs that do not bring them into contact with people or places that have a different experience. It is they who can be heard saying things like, 'The Troubles aren't as bad as the image portrayed on TV'; 'Watching the Northern Ireland news is depressing, so I don't watch it'; 'One side is as bad as the other;' and 'There are services out there to take care of people, and people make a lot of money out of compensation and are very comfortably off after big compensation settlements.'

In the other world, which we entered by doing this research, daily life is indeed suffused with experience of the Troubles. Certain things take on a significance that they don't have in the other dominant world. Driving to work every day, one begins to notice more and more the bunches of flowers on the roadside, which mark the sites of deaths in the Troubles. The calendar takes on a new significance, from January, and the anniversary of Bloody Sunday, to August and the anniversary of the Omagh bomb, then the realisation that, after thirty years, almost every day is an anniversary for someone. In the cities, certain streets are the sites of death. Some people can no longer go down a particular street, because a person they loved lay on that street in a pool of blood, or they themselves were attacked in that place.

In the first world, the Troubles are a news programme on a television that you can choose to turn off. In this other world, the Troubles become a voice in your head, reminding you that this is the very street, this is the very day so many years ago – and there is no on-off switch, the voice is constantly there, and the volume is often externally controlled. The Troubles are not an option. As Alice Nocher poignantly put it, 'The Troubles is my life.'

The process of conducting these interviews and working with the transcripts with our informants to the point of publication has allowed us to enter this other world to some extent. We are privileged not only by the insight we have gained in doing so, but also by the fact that we retain our place in that other world in which the Troubles are still an option. We can choose to research some other less demanding topic next time. Those we interview will remain living within the same unfolding personal story.

Thomas (1999) has described the tendency to regard those who have endured great suffering, notably Holocaust survivors, as 'moral beacons' in the wider world. Commonly, the assumption is made that those who have suffered are morally developed in some way by suffering, and can therefore offer moral leadership to the rest of us. This is a prevalent but not necessarily defensible view. Frankl's (1959) account of incarceration in the death camps of the Second World War describes how prisoners jeopardised other prisoners' lives in order to save themselves – a practice which Frankl sees as evidence of the extremity of the circumstances, and inherently human, though challenging to the mythology surrounding the moral integrity of the inmates of death camps. The experience of suffering is also used to explain subsequent violent behaviour. Crawford (1999) refers to the experience of Republican violence as a motivation for Loyalist paramilitary activity. He found that 30 per cent of the Loyalist prisoners he interviewed had 'members of their family' killed by the IRA/ Republicans – although he does not specify the degree of consanguinity between those killed and the prisoner. It seems that either great suffering is construed as motivating revenge or, if the sufferer manages to avoid being driven towards revenge, they are construed as having moral lessons to impart.

The idea that those who have suffered terribly have something to teach the rest of us is manifest, for example, by some of the media coverage of the Troubles. The past tendency of the media in Northern Ireland to ask immediate family members of a person killed in the Troubles if they forgive the perpetrator – often within hours or days of the death – can only be an attempt to signal, through the victim, to the wider society something about its own comparative state of forgiveness or blame. The bereaved person becomes a moral benchmark by which we can read off the degree of our own entitlement to anger, desire for revenge and impulses towards retaliation. The victim becomes a potential or actual moral beacon.

However, it seems suffering, alone, is not a sufficient qualification for such a role. The widow of the alleged informer, the victim of punishment beatings, or even the father of a prisoner are unlikely to qualify as moral beacons, in spite of their endurance of suffering. In order to qualify for this role, the suffering must be recognised as 'undeserved' according to dominant values. In deeply divided societies, attitudes to suffering are also divided; usually the suffering of one side is not easily recognised or acknowledged by the other. The production of a 'moral beacon' about which there is consensus is therefore problematic, since one side's suffering can be a source of the other side's triumph.

Gordon Wilson, whose daughter, Marie, was killed in the Enniskillen bomb was perhaps the best example of a moral beacon in the recent history of Northern Ireland. He was forgiving of his daughter's killers, and conciliatory in his political attitudes, accepting a seat in the Irish Senate. Yet in accepting a seat in the Irish Senate he compromised his position as a moral figure for sections of the Loyalist community.

The difficulties of consensus about morality – let alone politics – make the production of universal moral beacons problematic in Northern Ireland, yet one can see the tendency in spite of this. Such figures are often held up to us, implicitly or explicitly, to point to some higher state that we should strive for, some feat of self-transformation that we should attempt to achieve. Whilst those whose stories appear in this book may lead us to marvel at the resilience of the human spirit, we can also perhaps see something of ourselves in each one of them, diverse and divided as they are. In an increasingly divided world, we are ever more aware that armed conflict can break out where it is least expected. The accounts in this book show what that outbreak, and the sustained waging of such conflict, does to the lives of ordinary people. If they seem extraordinary, perhaps it is because of the catalytic effect of extraordinary events on ordinary lives, or perhaps it is the contrast between our lives and those described here. And perhaps it is because these accounts of events are not usually part of the official record, that history is often 'history from above' – or maybe even history without a divided and complicated heart.

REFERENCES

Crawford, C. (1999) *Defenders or Criminals? Loyalist Prisoners and Criminalisation.* Belfast: Blackstaff Press.
Frankl, V. (1959) *Man's Search for Meaning.* Boston: Beacon Press.
Thomas, L.M. (1999) 'Suffering as a Moral Beacon: Blacks and Jews' in Flanzbaum, H. (ed.) *The Americanization of the Holocaust.* Baltimore: Johns Hopkins.
Thompson, E.P. (1963) *The Making of the English Working Class.* London: Gollancz.

Appendix

We embarked on a series of in-depth interviews with a cross-section of people throughout Northern Ireland, which were to serve a number of functions. First, they were to provide qualitative data on the range and diversity of people's experience of the Troubles. Second, they were to provide subjective assessments of the effects of the Troubles on the range of people interviewed. Third, they were to form the basis for the questionnaire design, which was to be used in a subsequent survey.

In Northern Ireland, 'people affected by the violence' is not a homogeneous group: people have been affected in different ways and have different needs as a result. To collect detailed qualitative illustrations of the diversity and range of experience and needs of those affected by the Troubles, we conducted sixty-three in-depth interviews with men and women, old and young, Catholic, and Protestant from various parts of Northern Ireland. These interviews provide a wide variety of personal stories of experiences in the Troubles.

SELECTION OF INTERVIEWEES

In selecting interviewees, we avoided using the personal contacts of the researchers. We chose instead to use the contacts and suggestions from a range of people, some of whom were working in this field, and some were not. We asked them to nominate people that they thought should be interviewed, in order to achieve the goal of collecting a cross-section of experiences of the Troubles.

With the help of our own Board of Directors, other self-help groups, organisations and key individuals throughout Northern Ireland we recruited a group of interviewees from both communities, genders and a range of income groups. Once nominated, letters and information leaflets were sent to all the groups and individuals involved in nominating interviewees, informing them about the work of this study and asking them to identify individuals to be selected for interview. In these leaflets, we explained who we were, the purpose of the study, the way we handled consent and confidentiality. We offered people who were willing to participate in an interview the opportunity to tell their own story and be listened to carefully and respectfully.

Generally, this recruitment strategy was successful, although in the end, some organisations did not nominate anyone for interview. This appeared to be for organisational reasons, rather than any reluctance to cooperate. Only one organisation approached – an organisation for Loyalist prisoners – did not wish to cooperate, because they said that they were involved in doing their own research. Several organisations approached did not respond in spite of several reminders, and it is difficult to interpret this. possible explanations are the overburdened nature of many organisations in this field, or a lack of trust in us as a research project. Some organisations that cooperated presented us with other problems. One organisation, which nominated its employees for interview, seemed to us to have briefed its nominated interviewees before we interviewed them, and we got a 'party line' in response from all its nominated interviewees. These biased responses reduced the usefulness of the data considerably.

Whilst no set of interviews is going to be complete, we can clearly identify some gaps in the data that we failed to fill. In spite of several attempts through various channels to set up interviews with soldiers' families, or former soldiers, we did not succeed in obtaining interviews from this cohort. Conversely, in some areas where we were interviewing, people referred themselves for interview, they wanted to tell their stories. In these circumstances, we conducted the interview, even though we had not sought it. We took the view that the research and the researchers were committed to being responsive to the communities and individuals that we were working with. This happened in the case of four interviews out of the seventy we had conducted. It is interesting to note that none of these interviews added any significantly new material to our data set.

PROCEDURES USED IN QUALITATIVE DATA COLLECTION AND MANAGEMENT

Interviews were conducted by the Research Officer and the Project Director, both of whom are trained interviewers. Interviewees were provided with information about where to go for advice and help, apprised of voluntary groups that exist for people affected by the Troubles, and given a leaflet on self-help where appropriate.

Interviews were tape-recorded to broadcast quality. Each interview lasted approximately two and a half hours, and interviews ranged from fifty minutes to four hours in duration.

Consent

Before the tape-recorder was switched on, the issue of consent was discussed with the interviewees. Each interviewee was asked to complete a consent form on which was a written undertaking of confidentiality and anonymity. However, some interviewees wished their names to be used. The signing of the form signified that the interviewee understood and accepted the process taking place. This form asked interviewees to indicate with a tick:

(a) that they agree to be interviewed;
(b) that they are aware the interview is tape-recorded; and
(c) that they will be sent a full transcript of the interview and have the chance to make any changes to the transcript before it can be used in the research.

The interviewees were also given an undertaking that they would be shown the final version of the text of their interview before it was published and they would be consulted about photographs or images put alongside their interview in any publication or exhibition. This issue of confidentiality was regarded as a very important issue and the interviewees were guaranteed complete confidentiality. However, interviewees were also given the option of having their names used in any publication and some chose this option. By signing the consent form, interviewees acknowledged that they had been fully informed about the interviews and that they had been given information leaflets and a contact telephone number for the Cost of the Troubles Study. The interviewer also signed the form as a witness on behalf of the Cost of the Troubles Study. The interview data are not analysed or referred to in detail here, but were used to inform the design of the questionnaire. However, the interview data were used to prepare other publications and at each stage we went back to interviewees to obtain consent, as we were anxious not to increase our informants' sense of vulnerability. A small but significant number of interviewees withdrew their consent at various stages in this process. When this happened, the person's wishes were immediately respected without question, and we made no attempt to dissuade them from their decision. Those interviews, where they had taken place, were not used in the research.

Structure of Interviews

Interviews were semi-structured, in that interviewers, having ascertained certain demographic facts about the interviewee, namely age group, gender, marital status, location and perceived politico-religious identification, asked three basic questions. Interviewees were asked, 'What is your experience of the Troubles?' Interviewees were shown a time-line, indicating birth, childhood, teenage years and present age, and asked to review their entire experience in the light of the time-line. Interviewees were then asked, 'How do you think the Troubles have affected you?', although some of the effects of the Troubles may have already emerged in the answer to the first question. On both these questions, interviewees were prompted to answer broadly, not just the most traumatic experiences of the Troubles, but early experiences, not just the emotional effects, but the financial, educational, attitudinal effects also. Finally, interviewees were asked how they imagine their lives would have been different if the Troubles had not taken place. In retrospect, this last question was not as useful (or crucial) as the first two, and a significant number of interviewees had difficulty in answering it.

Distress in Interviews

We anticipated that some interviewees would become distressed in the course of interviews, and put in place arrangements for linking interviewees with supportive services should the need arise. Otherwise, the response made to distress on the part of the interviewee was simply to listen sympathetically, and remain with the interviewee until they had recovered some degree of equilibrium. About mid-way through conducting the interviews, it became clear that some interviewees, particularly those who were living with considerable emotional effects of the Troubles, found the process of being interviewed useful in some way. Some interviewees reported this to us, and associates of interviewees approached us wishing to be interviewed. We had also anticipated that the interviews would be distressing to the interviewers, and this proved to be the case. Formal and informal debriefing of interviewers formed part of the project work. Nonetheless, both interviewers report lasting effects from conducting the interviews.

Confidentiality and Anonymity

Standard practices of confidentiality and anonymity had to be amended to ensure that the interviewee's identity was concealed, in cases where they wished it to be concealed. In some cases, interviewees divulged information that would be legally or morally impossible to publish, such as naming people allegedly involved in acts of violence who had never been convicted. In such cases we negotiated with the interviewee so that we did not end up holding such information. A selection of interviews were edited into 'poems' which were then used in our exhibition, 'Do You Know What's Happened?', which has toured a number of venues. Other issues arose in the collection of qualitative data, which will be dealt with in more depth in other publications.

Coping Strategies

Sometimes it was neither ethical nor emotionally possible to walk away from people we interviewed without responding in some way to their story, or offering them some further information or contact. We had to maintain ongoing contact with interviewees during the period of transcription until the final transcript was agreed. In this period, we put a number of people in touch with self-help organisations or other services. One or two interviewees visited our offices, and we provided them with information about our work. Being able to offer helpful information or contacts in this way was helpful to us in dealing with our feelings of powerlessness in the face of the suffering of many of our interviewees. Another reaction to the involvement in this work was our growing identification with the 'victim' population, and beginning to engage in advocacy on behalf of the population as a whole with government organisations and NGOs (non-government organisations).

Debriefing was also an important formal coping strategy, where both interviewers participated in regular debriefing outside the project structures with people who had experience in this field. Within the office, the atmosphere was such that if someone came back from completing an interview, tea was made and the interviewer could discuss the experience with other staff as a way of immediately debriefing.

Feedback from early dissemination work, and from interviewees was also important to the morale of the project workers. A number of interviewees and others have told us that they regard our work as important and valuable, and that has been important to us in maintaining our commitment and keeping the work in perspective. At times when the level of violence rose, we were constantly news watching, and there were times when we had to face the possibility that we might not be able to complete the study as we had designed it. However, our difficulties were and are so little in comparison to those faced by those we have worked with, that this perspective provided the motivation and energy for continuing.

We have concentrated on those who have suffered as a result of the Troubles, and we have selected the most striking of the interviews for presentation here. The population of people affected by the Troubles is diverse. They are of both genders, all ages, religious beliefs and political persuasions. They are both guilty and innocent of having themselves caused death and destruction to their fellow citizens. We have selected interviews which we hope reflect some of that diversity.

Index

Compiled by Auriol Griffith-Jones